BRUTUS
AND OTHER
HEROINES

Also by Harriet Walter

Facing It
*Reflections on Images
of Older Women*

Macbeth
Actors on Shakespeare

Other People's Shoes
Thoughts on Acting

BRUTUS AND OTHER HEROINES

Playing Shakespeare's Roles for Women

HARRIET WALTER

NICK HERN BOOKS
London
www.nickhernbooks.co.uk

A Nick Hern Book

Brutus and Other Heroines first published in Great Britain in 2016 by Nick Hern Books Limited, The Glasshouse, 49a Goldhawk Road, London W12 8QP

Copyright © 2016 Harriet Walter

Harriet Walter has asserted her moral right to be identified as the author of this work

Designed and typeset by Nick Hern Books, London

Front cover image: © John Spinks
Back cover image: *Antony and Cleopatra* (RSC, 2006)
© Pascal Molliere/RSC
Author photo: © Georgia Oetker

Printed and bound in Great Britain by
Ashford Colour Press, Gosport, Hampshire

A CIP catalogue record for this book is available from the British Library

ISBN 978 1 84842 293 3

MIX
Paper from
responsible sources
FSC
www.fsc.org   FSC® C011748

Contents

Introduction

A part we have played is like a person we once met, grew to know, became intimately enmeshed with and finally moved away from. Some of these characters remain friends, others are like ex-lovers with whom we no longer have anything in common. All of them bring something out in us that will never go back in the box.

In this book I write about the major Shakespeare characters I have played. This sometimes involved revisiting pieces I had written much earlier in my life and my career, and doing this was a bit like looking back through old diaries with a mixture of affection and embarrassment. In reworking these pieces, I have deliberately preserved references that place our productions in a particular time (e.g. in Chapter Four on Imogen, I mention Glasnost; in Chapter Three on Portia, I refer to President Ronald Reagan), and I have stuck to the original thoughts I was wanting to convey, even if that meant exposing the naivety or idealism of my younger self.

Apart from the chapters on Ophelia, Imogen and Lady Macbeth, which are abridged or edited versions of pieces that had been published elsewhere, all the material has been freshly written this year. Younger characters have been recollected in tranquillity or written up from early essays or rehearsal notes. I had never written anything about Beatrice or Cleopatra before, and enjoyed reawakening those parts played fourteen and ten years ago respectively.

The last chapters of the book deal with still-current roles: the male protagonists in Phyllida Lloyd's all-female Shakespeare trilogy for the Donmar Warehouse. At the time of writing, we are reviving the two plays we have already performed (*Julius Caesar* and *Henry IV*) and are rehearsing the third (*The Tempest*). Here, the writing task is different. Obviously there is no difficulty in recalling details, but instead I have to step back, freeze the still flowing ideas about a part, and attempt to crystallise something that will have changed by the time you read this.

Many people suppose that we actors just have very vivid imaginations that carry us away until we believe we are someone else, and that all we then have to do is to remember the lines and not bump into the furniture. What is less understood is how we build a character through interpreting the text, and how we bring that character to life in collaboration with the director and the rest of the cast.

Much of acting work is about choices: the choices of interpretation and emphasis in rehearsing a role, and the minute-to-minute choices we make in response to an audience in performance. My choices will never be the same as someone else's, and if there were a right way and a wrong way to play a part we would all try to copy some 'definitive' performance, and life would be very dull. So this book is not intended as a blueprint to be followed to the letter, but I hope that it shows the sort of questions an actor needs to ask him- or herself in preparing a role, and how Shakespeare's text can be excavated for clues to support several interpretations. The important thing is that the character should be coherent with the play and production that surrounds it.

Two things happened to encourage me to write about playing Shakespeare. One was that, during my first seasons at the Royal Shakespeare Company in the 1980s, there existed a strong connection between the company and the

Shakespeare Institute, a department of Birmingham University, based in Stratford-upon-Avon. The Institute produced the collections called *Players of Shakespeare* (Cambridge University Press), in which RSC actors were invited to contribute a chapter on the particular character they were playing that season (see Chapter Four on Imogen). Here was an academic institution taking actors' insights seriously. They introduced the now totally accepted idea that, since Shakespeare wrote his plays to be performed and watched rather than studied, the players could make a valid contribution to the analysis of his works.

Secondly, around that same time, myself and four other leading actresses were interviewed by Professor Carol Rutter of Warwick University for her book *Clamorous Voices* (The Women's Press, 1988). She was interested in gathering the reactions and opinions of a generation of actresses who were bringing a new feminist experience to the famous female roles. I had taken my feminism for granted, not really knowing how these roles had been interpreted before, and Carol's book encouraged me to believe there was something fresh I could bring to the discussion.

This is not an academic book, nor is it a practical handbook. It is more personal than both of those. Perhaps it is a kind of autobiography in that it journeys from my thoughts as a thirty-year-old who understood the vulnerability of Ophelia, gaining confidence and complexity through my thirties and forties with Helena, Viola, Portia and Lady Macbeth, to a more relaxed, womanly Beatrice and Cleopatra in my fifties, and onward to finding new territory in the male roles in my sixties. As with any autobiography, I can impose a retrospective shape on a life that was experienced in a more blinkered present tense. Perhaps this is my attempt to lay down a record of an art form that is only true in the moment of performance.

August 2016

Acknowledgements

I want to thank the many directors who have given me such heady opportunities, passed on their insights and helped build and develop my courage as a performer of Shakespeare over so many years; in particular John Barton, Richard Eyre, Trevor Nunn, Greg Doran and Phyllida Lloyd.

A huge thank-you to Faith Evans, whom I first met as editor of *Clamorous Voices*, and who then became my literary agent, encouraging me to write my first book, *Other People's Shoes*. Thanks also to Matt Applewhite and everyone at Nick Hern Books, who have benignly nagged me while I procrastinated in writing this book, and especially to Nick Hern himself, who reissued *Other People's Shoes*, and saved me from many writing pitfalls while editing this book.

*

Photo credits: Ophelia in *Hamlet* © John Haynes/Lebrecht Music & Arts; Helena in *All's Well That Ends Well* by Reg Wilson, Lady Macbeth in *Macbeth* by Jonathan Dockar-Drysdale, and Cleopatra in *Antony and Cleopatra* by Pascal Molliere, all © RSC; Portia in *The Merchant of Venice* by John Peters; Imogen in *Cymbeline* and Viola in *Twelfth Night*, both © Ivan Kyncl/ArenaPAL; Beatrice in *Much Ado About Nothing* © Donald Cooper/Photostage; Brutus in *Julius Caesar* and King Henry IV in *Henry IV*, both © Helen Maybanks. Every effort has been made to trace copyright holders, but if any have been inadvertently overlooked, the publisher will be pleased to make the necessary arrangements at the first opportunity.

Acknowledgements

OPHELIA
A Case Study

As Ophelia with Jonathan Pryce (Hamlet)
Hamlet, Royal Court Theatre, London, 1980

This piece is taken from my book Other People's Shoes, *which I wrote in 1998. It came in a chapter in which I was specifically demonstrating the psychological approach to a character. I wrote it up from jotted notes I had made while rehearsing several years earlier in 1980. It was my first professional Shakespeare role but not the first I wrote about. This was a thrilling, ground-breaking production to be a part of, and Ophelia proved to be a stepping stone towards my understanding of how to approach character through language.*

Sometimes, when one role is offered hot on the heels of another, your imagination remains so steeped in the world of the last role that it spills over into the next. When Richard Eyre asked me to play Ophelia to Jonathan Pryce's Hamlet at the Royal Court, he had just finished directing me in a film for television called *The Imitation Game* by Ian McEwan. This was the story of a young woman, Cathy Raine, who joined the army in the Second World War and was posted to the code-breaking head-quarters at Bletchley. She was bright and well educated but soon realised that her talents were to be buried in menial tasks cleaning up after the Cambridge boffins. Her frustration and need to get near the centre of things resulted in her being imprisoned for the duration of the war as a suspected spy.

The piece was a brilliant exposé of patriarchal double standards, and before starting work on it Richard Eyre suggested I read Virginia Woolf's essay *Three Guineas*. This was one of her last works before she committed suicide in 1941. It is an agonisingly relentless analysis of the patriarchal imperative to war and the way in which women collude with it. Woolf looked straight into the light alone and was burned up by it. At the end of *The Imitation Game* Cathy Raine has seen a similar light but lacks Woolf's tools to articulate it. Locked up, suicidal or tipped into madness, that was the fate of women who, had they lived now, would have been buoyed up by a tumultuous sisterly chorus.

With these things still churning in my mind, I started to tackle Ophelia. Fresh from *The Imitation Game* himself, Richard was also working on some kind of continuum of themes: patriarchal power, secrecy, corrupted love, the destruction of a woman. His version of Elsinore carried echoes of the corridors of Whitehall. Geoffrey Chater's patrician Polonius would have been perfectly at home in MI5, and to reinforce the connection, he had played the witheringly steely colonel who had locked me up in *The Imitation Game*. Ophelia was to be no flibberty damsel, but an intelligent girl locked in her mind by the oppressive rules of the establishment.

The Royal Court's brief was to put on new plays or, if it did do any classics, to rework or reinterpret them as if they were new plays. Richard had wanted to emphasise the modern political play in *Hamlet*, and to this end he chose to eschew the supernatural element. His most controversial decision was to cut the part of Hamlet's father's ghost. The reason for this was that unlike Shakespeare's audience, we no longer believed in Heaven and Hell as actual places, nor in tormented spirits trapped between the two. Instead of

Hamlet's father's ghost being an outward manifestation visible and audible to whoever was on watch that night, he was to be understood as a projection of Hamlet's fevered mind. Hamlet was possessed by his father's spirit. When his father 'visited' him, Jonathan Pryce's body writhed and contorted as if some alien creature had invaded him and was kicking at his sides. He belched the ghost's words from the pit of his stomach and gasped for air as his own voice recovered enough to answer.

Richard's 'modern play' approach helped ease me into what was my first classical role. Before I came across John Barton and Cicely Berry at the RSC, who both taught me so much about creating character through language, I could think of no other way to approach Ophelia than through her psychology. We had a mere three-and-a-half weeks to rehearse, which meant that if I were lucky I would get about two shots at each scene before the run-throughs and technical rehearsals began. I was timid and apologetic about taking up rehearsal time, so inevitably I did a lot of my work at home.

The most famous thing about Ophelia is that she goes mad. Richard had given me one major tip as to what he wanted, by telling me what he *didn't* want. He did not want 'mad acting'. I knew what he meant. For Ophelia, her mad scene is an ungoverned artless release; for the actress playing her it can be a chance to show off her repertoire of lolling tongues and rolling eyes, in a fey and affecting aria which is anything but artless. That is the paradox of acting mad. The actor is self-conscious in every sense, while the mad person has lost their hold on self.

Generalised mad acting, being unhinged from any centre, leaves the actor floundering in their own embarrassment. The remedy for me was to find a method in Ophelia's madness, so that I could root her actions in her motivations (however insane and disordered), just as I would with any other character I was playing. Before playing her I had shared with many others the impression that Ophelia was a bit of a colourless part—that is, until she goes mad. I needed to find a unifying scheme that would contain both the 'interesting' mad Ophelia and the 'boring' sane Ophelia.

Suppose Ophelia is happily 'normal' until her lover rejects her and murders her father. Is that necessarily a cue to go mad? After all, Juliet suffered something of the kind when Romeo killed Tybalt, and although the idea tormented her she did not flip. I started to see that the seeds of Ophelia's madness had been sown long before the play started, by the workings of a cold, repressive environment on an already susceptible mind. I preferred this theory to the sudden-madness-through-grief idea which, together with broken hearts and walking spirits, seemed to belong in the theatre of Henry Irving or a Victorian poem.

In the little time available to me, I scoured the libraries for modern clinical accounts of madness and found much to latch on to in R.D. Laing's *Sanity, Madness and the Family* and *The Divided Self*. I am not concerned here with the pros and cons of Laing's approach; what interested me were his case histories of young schizophrenic women, and the mechanisms by which their families inadvertently contributed to their disorder. A latent schizophrenic tendency need not necessarily develop into madness, but certain triggers might set it off.

Here I found some uncanny Elsinore echoes. They always say Shakespeare can be made to fit any argument, but in this case I suppose it was just further proof that he knew all there was to know about human nature. If he had been directing me, he would no doubt have been impatient with my approach. 'Just say the lines, love,' he might have said. 'I promise it will work.' It was my own imagination that needed to do more. So with Shakespeare, Laing and Virginia Woolf to help me, I built my little theory.

From some of my jottings at the time

Family: father Polonius, brother Laertes. Mother is dead and no one mentions her. No known female companion. Only female role model known to be present in her life is Gertrude, who has too many of her own problems to be much help.

Speculation

Little experience of love. Duty rather than deep love binds her to her father, and although her brother had been an affectionate companion in childhood, they have been brought up increasingly apart from one another. Her education, such as it is, has been mostly at her father's hands and of a deliberately unworldly nature, while her brother's education was a serious preparation for a public role in life.

Clues in the text

All in the name of loving protection, Laertes undermines Ophelia's trust in Hamlet and '*the trifling of his favour*'. '*You must fear,*' he tells her. '*Fear it, Ophelia, fear it my dear sister.*' And in case she still hasn't got it, '*Be wary.*' Layer upon layer he adds, talking of '*the danger of desire*' and her '*too credent ear*'. On departing, Laertes charges her to '*Remember well what I have said to you,*' and Ophelia replies, ''*Tis in my memory locked, and you yourself shall keep the key of it.*' Yet the very next minute, when Polonius pounces in with, '*What is't Ophelia he hath said to you?*', she replies, '*So please you, something touching the lord Hamlet,*' and within seconds she is spilling it all out. So much for locked-up secrets.

To keep a secret is a means of preserving the self. It is proof to the keeper that they own a private self that cannot be reached. One of Laing's cases 'found it difficult to keep anything to herself because she talked too much and besides she thought people could read her thoughts'.

Further quotes from R.D. Laing's patients

One woman spoke of her father, who kept worrying 'that I should be kidnapped or some dreadful thing happen to me. It's my own fault. He's got no confidence in me at all. I am always going to be led away by some crafty cunning bad man. He has put that into my mind, he has got that impregnated into my brain in some way.'

'I am not supposed to have an opinion because my opinion is bound to be incorrect you know... Perhaps my opinion isn't what you call reliable, perhaps in every way I am not reliable. I feel that I have to accept that I am not reliable.'

I know there is a danger in too schematic an approach to acting, particularly Shakespeare, and that I could easily have been carried off course by the sheer fun of theory-building, so I made sure that I took from Laing only what I needed, and relied on Shakespeare and events in the rehearsal room for the rest. The exercise was not about diagnosing Ophelia as a schizophrenic, but about gaining insight into the text. I started to hear the other characters' words from Ophelia's point of view, as traps and ambushes, and as means of controlling her mind.

'*To thine own self be true*,' Polonius advises Laertes as he sees him off on his travels, while in the same scene he tells Ophelia, '*You do not understand yourself.*' Young men should learn to fend for themselves in life's battles, gaining confidence through experience, whereas women must be kept in fear and ignorance of their very natures.

Ophelia submits to another battering from Polonius: '*Do not believe his vows... Affection? Pooh! You speak like a green girl.*' He asks her, '*Do you believe his tenders, as you call them?*', and to Ophelia's simple reply, '*I do not know, my lord, what I should think,*' he answers, '*Marry, I shall teach you: think yourself a baby.*' He does such a good job on her that by the end of the scene Ophelia has promised to reject Hamlet, send back all his letters and never speak to him again.

Other Shakespeare heroines have fought back under like circumstances. Jessica defies Shylock and runs off with Lorenzo. Rosalind, Imogen and Julia risk punishment and banishment in search of true love, but a lifetime of indoctrination, together with a particularly impressionable nature, ensures that Ophelia cannot resist.

From that moment on she puts herself entirely in her father's hands. Having been terrified by an encounter with the seemingly deranged Hamlet, rather than try to talk to him, she rushes to her father and blurts out the whole story. Polonius in his turn reports everything back to the King, and all this culminates in the plot to test Hamlet's madness in which Ophelia is quite wittingly used as bait. Guilt, love, duty and, above all, terror confound her. Given this state of affairs, imagine the following exchanges from Ophelia's point of view.

(*Ophelia offers to return Hamlet's gifts.*)

HAMLET: I never gave you aught.

OPHELIA: My honour'd lord, you know right well you did…

(*Which of them is going crazy?*)

HAMLET: Are you honest?

OPHELIA: My lord?

HAMLET: Are you fair?

OPHELIA: What means your lordship?

HAMLET: That if you be honest and fair, your honesty should admit no discourse to your beauty.

OPHELIA: Could beauty, my lord, have better commerce than with honesty?

(*Holding her own pretty well; but then…*)

HAMLET: Ay, truly. For the power of beauty will sooner transform honesty from what it is to a bawd than the force of honesty can translate beauty into his likeness. This was sometime a paradox, but now the time gives it proof. I did love you once.

OPHELIA: Indeed, my lord, you made me believe so.

HAMLET: You should not have believed me… I loved you not.

OPHELIA: I was the more deceived.

This would be pretty devastating to most of us, but Ophelia is disintegrating fast. I am trying to convey something of the sensation of playing Ophelia, given the story so far.

When Hamlet suddenly springs on Ophelia, '*Where's your father?*', the girl who cannot keep a secret feels transparent and replies, '*At home, my lord*', a little too quickly. She has blown the cover, and now that Hamlet has seen through the plot, she is powerless to dissociate herself from its cynical perpetrators. She puts up little resistance as Hamlet brutally rejects her, in a scene played out mostly for the ears of her eavesdropping puppet-masters.

When everyone has left the stage, Ophelia gives us her one soliloquy that ends with, '*O woe is me, to have seen what I have seen, see what I see!*' The line has a similar ring to Isabella's in *Measure for Measure*:

To whom should I complain? Did I tell this,
Who would believe me?

The audience has witnessed the abuse of both women and is on their side, but the women themselves cannot be reached or helped. They are sealed in the world of the play, with a knowledge that is too dangerous to share. The big difference is that Isabella has a gigantic sense of her self and her integrity while Ophelia has virtually none. She has depended on Hamlet and her brother and father for what flimsy self-definition she has. The one has just denounced her as a whore, the second is abroad and the third is about to be murdered by the first.

I am not going to start decoding Ophelia's ramblings in the mad scene, because that is a task for each actress who plays her. How much does she know? Did she sleep with Hamlet? These and many other questions are up for grabs. The important thing is to work out your own private coherence and to have a strong intention behind each thing you say. However broken up your story, let each fragment come from a clear image. If there are 'unconscious' tics, let them come from a centred impulse. Inhabit your world, don't demonstrate it.

With a director who is sympathetic to your intentions, any demonstrating can be done for you by the production itself. Out of sheer embarrassment I never disclosed the details of my homework to Richard Eyre, but the tentative sketch that I brought to rehearsals gave him at least enough to go on. He picked up Ophelia's message, however faint, and helped to focus it physically. His greatest gift to me came in the shape of props.

The first was a bundle of Hamlet's letters upon which my grasp weakened as the play progressed. In the first scene I clung to them as if they embodied my faith in Hamlet, only to surrender them to Polonius as soon as he beckoned me to. In Act III, Scene 1, Polonius placed the letters in my lap like a photographer arranging a picture. He and Claudius have staged the scene, and the letters are Ophelia's props. She hands them to Hamlet, saying:

> My lord, I have remembrances of yours
> That I have longéd long to redeliver.
> I pray you now receive them.

As Hamlet departs at the end of the scene, he throws the letters in Ophelia's face, and they scatter on the floor. Claudius and Polonius re-emerge from their listening-post and discuss the scene they have just witnessed as if Ophelia were not in the room. She, meanwhile, crawls around the floor gathering up the letters as though they were the shards of her life.

The second prop that helped to tell my story was a bundle of blackened twigs. These were a memorable substitute for Ophelia's usual picturesque garlands. This not only added to her delusion but somehow helped to suggest a subversiveness, a sense that she knew something. *'Follow her close. Give her good watch, I pray you,'* says Claudius. She is dangerous not just to herself but to the court. When I presented Claudius with a gnarled stick saying, *'Here's fennel for you and columbines,'* it was no pretty gift but an accusation.

My performance fell far short of my aims, mainly because I was inexperienced and too inhibited to carry out all that I had planned at home, but I was totally supported by the production. Bill Dudley's set, with its secret panels and *trompe l'œil* life-sized 'spies' lurking in the corners, together with a soundtrack of indecipherable whisperings, all added to the atmosphere of paranoia, and the chamber scale of the Royal Court suited my implosive rather than explosive version of madness.

But could I have been explosive if I'd wanted to be? That was the next question, put to me (in slightly different terms) by Trevor Nunn, who had seen my Ophelia and was sizing me up for the part of Helena in *All's Well That Ends Well.* He had appreciated the detail of my performance but, as he put it, could I preserve that detail and reach the back of the auditorium? (Bear in mind that he was talking main house at Stratford, not the cosy Royal Court.) Luckily for me, Trevor took the risk, and over the next decade I joined in the effort to combine intimacy with projection, heightened language with naturalistic speech, and verbal dexterity with physical strength that has preoccupied the RSC since it first began.

HELENA
Heroine or Harpy?

As Helena with Peggy Ashcroft (Countess)
All's Well That Ends Well, Royal Shakespeare Company, 1981

In 1991 I was invited to give a paper on Women in Theatre at the Divina Conference at Turin University. I titled it 'The Heroine, the Harpy and the Human Being'. I wanted to look at the perceptions of virtue and vice in female characters and to uphold the right of women and female characters to be imperfect and flawed without being condemned as the baddy, the whore or the temptress.

The full piece dealt with modern as well as classical roles and was later published in New Theatre Quarterly (*Vol. IX, number 34*).

For this book I decided to focus on the character of Helena in All's Well That Ends Well, *who exemplifies many of my observations. In order to be true to what I was writing at the time, I have kept to these observations in the current reworking for this book, but I am happy to say that a lot of the attitudes I was up against then have changed.*

A more detailed study of Helena can be read in a piece I wrote for Clamorous Voices.

What is Virtue?

A ny actress playing a classical heroine has to tackle the concepts of virtue and chastity: they are words which come up so centrally and so often that it is impossible to skirt round them. They are used to define the whole woman, and often nothing else about her is known or deemed to be important. As a modern woman I could never connect personally with the significance the word 'chastity' had for a character I was playing, until Helena in *All's Well That Ends Well* showed me a way through. I found if I mentally substituted the word 'integrity' for 'chastity', I could reach her need to preserve her sense of self, her internal moral core.

According to the morality of the day, a woman was virtuous simply by being a virgin. A virgin was a commodity on the marriage market, and if a woman lost her virginity out of wedlock, she was sullied goods and lost all claim to virtue. Virtue and virginity became one and the same.

But this makes virtue passive, or at most something to be maintained by resisting, a negative action. This kind of virtue is a male-centred definition, to do with the value of a prize to be won by men, and nothing to do with the intrinsic moral worth of a female human being. In other words, in classical drama and literature men earn their worth through their actions, whereas a heroine doesn't have to do anything, she just has to *be* innocent, preferably quiet, and definitely a virgin. Female virtue is a state of being, rather than doing.

Historically, it was men who created the tie-up between a woman's virginity and her virtue, but we women want our heroines and ourselves to be tested against the general human virtues and prove ourselves by our deeds and decisions against the same criteria as men.

A Mingled Yarn

In Act IV, Scene 3, of *All's Well That Ends Well* Shakespeare says:

> The web of our life is of a mingled yarn, good and ill
> together: our virtues would be proud, if our faults
> whipped them not; and our crimes would despair, if they
> were not cherished by our virtues.

It is one of my favourite speeches. It is not at all famous and comes from the mouth of a minor character who doesn't even have a name (the First Lord).

It felt to me to be one of the central tenets of the play, and therefore it seemed that Shakespeare intended his chief female character, Helena, to reflect it. I believe Shakespeare deliberately created a heroine who is imperfect but whose worth he ultimately believes in. He challenges the audience to accept a flawed female as their guide through the story and to allow her to win in the end. That end remains ambiguous but, I think, hopeful. It would be unbelievable if it were all rosy, but it would be uncharacteristically cynical if the title were entirely ironic.

Helena came to me with a bad reputation. Critics over the years had judged her as immodest, ambitious, predatory and sanctimonious. It was 1981, and the play had not often been performed because so many people deemed it unplayable and the heroine unacceptable. What is Helena's crime? She pursues the man of her choice rather than waiting for him to choose her. Helena's namesake in *A Midsummer Night's Dream* (which I played in that same season) also chases after her man, but she is loveable because her quest is hopeless and it is treated comedically. In Act II, Scene 2, she voices the inappropriateness of her behaviour and despises her own desperation:

> We cannot fight for love, as men may do.
> We should be woo'd and were not made to woo,

and what is here comically expressed, is the predicament of the other, more serious Helena as well.

I was not interested in judging *All's Well*'s Helena. I had my work cut out learning her very opaque speeches and summoning the courage and technique to play my first major Shakespeare role on the main stage at Stratford in the company of Dame Peggy Ashcroft among other luminaries.

What I instantly related to was a woman of ambition. To date, my favourite role had been Nina in *The Seagull*. Nina is no ordinary sweet young thing but an ambitious actress eager for experience, who gets battered by tragedy, is strengthened by it and moves on. I could always relate to ambition, having plenty of drive myself. What was harder to relate to was the fact that the full extent of Helena's ambition was to get her man.

Precisely because she is hard to label, Helena is one of the most interesting and modern of Shakespeare's women that I have ever played. However, the label-seeking analysts want to know where they stand. They fret over whether *All's Well* is a comedy, a romance or a tragedy. The answer is that it hops between all three and all three overlap; a bit like life really. But a label it must have, so it becomes 'a problem play', and the major problem is what to make of the central couple, Helena and Bertram.

It is one thing to come to terms with a heroine who pursues and traps a man into marriage, but another to accept that the man she pursues doesn't seem worth the effort. Neither hero nor heroine is likeable.

The issue of likeability is one I have come up against often since, but never so clearly as with Helena. Seldom does anybody ask whether they *like* Hamlet, Henry V, or King Lear, but somehow the heroine has to be sympathetic, palatable, liked. It is definitely easier for a woman to be liked if she is pretty, gentle, and unassuming than if she is intense, ambitious, and complicated like Helena.

On the other hand, it is interesting that George Bernard Shaw preferred Helena to any other Shakespeare heroine, and having studied the part in depth and played it in repertoire over a period of two years, I feel certain that Shakespeare was basically on her side. Every decent, wise character in the play approves of her, and her only detractors are Parolles, a known cheat, and Bertram, an immature snobbish boy.

From the start, I felt for Helena's unrequited love and her social isolation. I liked her for her ambition and the way she shoved self-pity aside and followed her dream. I admired her guts chancing her arm at curing the King. I was fascinated by her oblique, broken-up, cryptic soliloquies at the beginning of the play. They gave me a clue as to her tangled thoughts, and the fact that she almost could not speak her ambition out loud, it seemed so transgressive. This means that she could barely admit her feelings to herself, since a confessional soliloquy to the audience is the equivalent of talking to oneself.

About her faults I was maybe less than honest. I was feeling defensive against what seemed to be a historical sea of prejudice, so I was perhaps in denial about any of her shortcomings, her possible underhandedness, her blinkeredness about Bertram's feelings, her scheming—and I sought every justification for these that I could dig out of the text.

Trevor Nunn, the director, also saw the need to redeem the misunderstood Helena if he was going to make the play work. By setting the play in the early twentieth century, he helped my interpretation of Helena by suggesting a connection with the emancipated heroines of Ibsen and Shaw. He also encouraged me to emphasise Helena's trepidation and thereby her bravery, to dig out and deliver whatever self-deprecatory wit she might have, and to find her moments of remorse and compassion for Bertram. The opportunities were all there in Shakespeare's text.

Yes, she can seem secretive and indirect, especially in her dealings with Bertram, but I put that down to diffidence and self-doubt. Yes, she can seem manipulative but, as I see it, she only manipulates what Fate seems to set in her pathway, and Fate seems consistently to reward her faith. First her pursuit of Bertram gets a blessing from his own mother, the Countess of Rousillon, then her faith (plus a little medical know-how) manages to cure the King of France of a fatal disease, and then the King promises her Bertram as her reward.

When things go terribly wrong and Helena realises that her monomania has driven Bertram away from France and on to the battlefield and possible death, she is willing to give up her pursuit, become a wandering pilgrim and leave France, since it is her presence there that has forced Bertram to run to the wars.

> No, come thou home, Rousillon,
> Whence honour but of danger wins a scar,
> As oft it loses all: I will be gone;
> My being here it is that holds thee hence:
> Shall I stay here to do't? no, no, although
> The air of paradise did fan the house
> And angels officed all: I will be gone.

All this seems quite clearly to indicate her willing self-sacrifice to Bertram's happiness, but then, for the sake of a good plot, Shakespeare has her winding up in Italy and, by 'coincidence', exactly in that part of Italy where Bertram's regiment is stationed. The prejudiced in the audience see only the schemer deliberately stalking her prey. They forget the soliloquy they have recently heard. Actions have spoken louder than words.

The fact that everyone Helena meets seems to like her, including the Widow and Diana, who take to her immediately, can be seen by the prejudiced as evidence of her manipulative charm. I tried to be as straight as possible, but the plot is twisty and doesn't help me.

Why did I try? Partly I was being true to what I found in the text, but partly I was guilty of wanting to make Helena as palatable as I possibly could. This tends to happen with actresses of my generation who do not want to play into any possible misogynist interpretations of a female role. We feel burdened by the need to overcompensate and make our character better than anyone else, wiser, more moral, more sympathetic; and that leads to a different, though understandable, kind of inaccuracy.

Helena was complicated enough for me not to have to come down one side or another of the 'heroine or harpy' argument. I loved her variety, her contradictions, her elusiveness, her switches from diffidence to dynamism, from conjuror to rejected victim, from pilgrim to adventurer. I love her 'feminine' empathy and her 'masculine' wooing and pursuing; and she does all this without having to wear trousers!

After a long and painful journey she wins through. Bertram has been through a painful journey too, and Helena's steadfastness, that once sickened him, becomes the very thing he needs to redeem him from his own self-loathing and humiliation.

I did have trouble with both Shakespeare's and Trevor's idea of the woman as redeemer. This kind of idealism doesn't seem true to a real woman's experience any more than the negative portrayal of a scheming succubus, but I also can't believe that Shakespeare meant to leave the audience with a sense of 'Well, *that* marriage sure ain't gonna last' or 'Poor geezer saddled with that domineering woman'. I think he meant to leave us with a feeling that these two people have gone on an incredible journey, and who knows? They might work it out, and their life could be very interesting.

Whatever *All's Well*'s textbook reputation, Shakespeare wrote it to be performed rather than read or written about, and, as we hoped it would prove, with the flesh and blood of live performance the harpy Helena and the wastrel Bertram were revealed to be human beings of a mingled yarn.

The production was received for the most part with rapture. The acting was praised, but I could not entirely enjoy the success. Despite all our efforts to clarify Helena's motives, one male critic still referred to her as 'the martyr/bitch'. Therefore I felt I had failed. Now, however, I'm inclined to think that that review told me more about the reviewer's fears than about my performance, and that the prejudice and misogyny of a few male critics is their problem, not mine. If, despite the delicate ambiguity we placed in the final moments of the play, one critic managed to read a 'triumphant smile' into my apprehensive face as I took Bertram's hand, and if, despite our leaving the audience with the tentative optimism we dared to believe that Shakespeare himself intended, some critics chose to read blatant cynicism into it, that is their right. What more could I do?

Like many of the women we portray, we actresses have become expert at the subtle, the subversive, and the almost subliminal means of communicating our beliefs. The trouble is that this indirectness leaves the door wide open for misinterpretation. One's personal statement obliquely infiltrated into a piece of work or a character is necessarily filtered through the eyes and ears of the beholder, and it is the beholder's right to understand it as he or she feels.

Whether in classical or modern drama, I fight for the right to portray women who are as contradictory, complex and diverse as the women I see all around me, and I uphold my right to present ordinary, flawed women at the heart of a play.

Virtue and its opposite are human, not an endowment from the gods. There is always a chink in the halo, or a redeeming shaft of light under the black hood. As an actor you look for your character's motive. That is almost all you have to know. You try to understand why they do what they do and then set the acting in motion. We do not sit in judgment at the centre of our character any more than we spend our day assessing our own character at every moment of our lives in the real world. Whether the part I am playing is deemed a heroine or a harpy, I only need concern myself with her thoughts, her words and her deeds—and by following them I find a complex human being.

PORTIA, VIOLA (& IMOGEN)
A Year of Playing Boys

As Portia
The Merchant of Venice
Royal Exchange Theatre, Manchester, 1987

In 1987 I was asked to play Portia in The Merchant of Venice *at the Royal Exchange in Manchester and to follow that up with a season at the RSC in Stratford and London playing Viola in* Twelfth Night *and Imogen in* Cymbeline. *So I decided to write about playing the girls who play boys, as all three of them do. I hadn't done any Shakespeare since the 1981–3 RSC season in which I had played Helena in Trevor Nunn's production of* All's Well That Ends Well, *and after a decent spell of television and contemporary theatre I felt ready for another season of classics.*

From the start I was intent on finding the differences between all three characters as I did not want to repeat myself. My worry was that perhaps there was only one boy in me, but I came to see that Shakespeare had given each girl a very distinct nature and a very different reason for their disguise. Initially the piece covered all three girls, but for this book, I have cut the section on Imogen because I was subsequently commissioned to write about her separately (see the following chapter).

This was my first piece of writing on playing Shakespeare. It came from an invitation to write for a publication that never materialised, but, not having written anything since my schooldays, I decided to take up the challenge. I have reshaped it for this book but have preserved my original thoughts.

Portia/Balthasar

Funny to think Shakespeare never expected that a woman would ever play Juliet, or Cleopatra, or Portia.

We are working in a live art-form, as was Shakespeare. We try to 'talk' to Shakespeare, to dig back through the centuries to reach the original germ that motivated Shakespeare to write and which still moves us to perform his works. So we ask, 'What did Shakespeare mean?' and in asking this question a woman meets an obstacle: 'He never meant *you* to play the part.'

Shakespeare wrote to the strengths of his company, so a modern actress's expectations in the Shakespearean repertoire could be said to be proscribed by the limitations or excellences of two or three generations of Elizabethan boy players. Although many young male actors specialised in female roles and never played men, it is likely that others played the female roles during their apprenticeship before graduating to the male roles. I am grateful for that because, although they were junior in status within the company (and probably kept that way by the older actors), I don't see much evidence that less acting ability was demanded of them by William Shakespeare. The verse is as dense and as beautiful, the emotional depth as great, the wit as brilliant (frequently more so), the psychology as complex in Shakespeare's female characters as in the male.

It may be that since today's Ophelia might be tomorrow's Hamlet and a possible manager of the company, there was a vested interest in stretching his capabilities to the utmost. Judging by attitudes towards female players when they did come along a century or so later, it is quite possible that if he had been writing for women, Shakespeare would have tailored the female roles to fit the accepted limits of female decorum and would have produced a much narrower range of characters for us to tackle; so again I am thankful.

In some ways these quirks of social history that helped shape Shakespeare's plays have given me a rare gift, but they have also limited the quantity of those gifts. I imagine that boy players quickly passed their prime of prettiness and graduated to playing men. So another consequence of social history is that modern actresses lack the continuum of female roles on up through the range of ages which would sustain us in an ever enriching and demanding career such as some of my male counterparts enjoy.

But enough of this. I am currently enjoying my prime while it is with me, and I rarely forget how exceptionally lucky I am. I have been offered three 'trouser roles' in one year, so 1987 is the Year of the Boy for me. I need to differentiate between them. I ask these questions: Why did they disguise as boys? How does their disguise change other characters around them? Do they enjoy their own disguise? What do they learn from it? Each character answers differently, and I want to make use of these differences so that each play might teach me something new and explore something unknown in myself.

The year began with Portia. *The Merchant of Venice* is often labelled an anti-Semitic play and, as its heroine, the same accusation has been levelled at Portia. I am puzzled by this. There is a big difference between a play that depicts an anti-Semitic society and an inherently racist play. Ben Jonson famously described Shakespeare as a man *'for all time'*, but he was also a man of his own historical time, so he sometimes comes up with attitudes which we now find hard to accept. I don't want to get too hooked up on this argument, but I would say, firstly, that Shakespeare's audience are unlikely to have known what anti-Semitism was as there were only a negligible number of Jews living in England at the time, and, secondly, that Shakespeare's portrait of Shylock is largely sympathetic and famously emphasises our common humanity:

Hath not a Jew eyes?

Is a Jew not

> fed with the same food, hurt with the same weapons,
> subject to the same diseases, healed by the same means,
> warmed and cooled by the same winter and summer, as a
> Christian is?

And Shakespeare seems very modern in his understanding that abuse leads to abuse when he has Shylock say:

> If a Jew wrong a Christian, what is his humility? Revenge.
> If a Christian wrong a Jew, what should his sufferance be
> by Christian example? Why, revenge. The villainy you
> teach me, I will execute.

To me it seems that if Shakespeare is on anyone's side it is Shylock's, but he also wants us to love Portia. The only thing that can possibly be construed as racist in Portia is that, in the trial scene, she upholds the law of Venice, which was a Christian, and therefore an inherently anti-Jewish, law. I tried hard to play this as a troubling rather than a triumphant moment for Portia, not because I wanted to whitewash her but because Shakespeare's play can only work in its entirety if we approve of Portia. Therefore I made some little adjustments of emphasis where I could, so as to avoid alienating a twentieth-century audience. I worked on the premise that Shakespeare intended Portia to be a generous spirit, containing the hope for the future. To work against that is to undermine the final act and the spirit of the play.

In the production I did in Manchester, the director Braham Murray, himself a Jew, realised that by putting a lot of focus on to the triangular love story of Antonio, Bassanio and Portia, he could unlock some of the impasse in which the play has left our post-Holocaust sensitivities. He posited very plausibly that the title, *The Merchant of Venice*, suggests that it was not Shylock but Antonio who was intended as the central character. Shylock only came into the plot because the economy of sixteenth-century Venice depended on moneylenders, and these were invariably Jews. Shylock was/is part of a subplot that connected the idea of bonds of love to that of financial bonds, but as Shakespeare developed him, he became the richly human character that is considered one of the greatest roles in the canon, attracting all the great actors through history to play him and thereby tipping Shylock into the central role.

In our production he was played by a great old Norwegian actor, Espen Skjønberg who, although he in no way softened the danger in the man, could not avoid giving off a humanity and warmth that had the audience eating out of his hand. The actors playing the Christians in Venice did not avoid the vanity and anti-Semitism they found in the text, and the trial scene was cruel and terrifying. These factors all militated against any perceived anti-Semitism that might obstruct the audience's way to the heart of the play. Indeed in Manchester, which has a large Jewish population, Espen reported that several people, including two rabbis, had approached him in the street and thanked him for his sympathetic portrayal.

For my own part, as Portia, I tried to show a woman of great spirit and intelligence trapped by her father into a waiting game. Her father's will forces her to wait for a husband until a suitor chooses the right casket out of three. As she watches these men going through their hoops, we see Portia as volatile and impatient, and no suitor escapes her barbed tongue. One by one, the suitors choose wrongly and reveal their vanity and shallowness, and Portia grows in her understanding of men. She begins to accept her father's wisdom. Maybe he was right, as her sidekick Nerissa suggests: '*Holy men at their death have good inspirations…*' Maybe her father knew that the right casket '*will, no doubt, never be chosen by any rightly but one who shall rightly love*'.

In Portia's eyes, when Bassanio chooses the right casket, these words are vindicated. Papa was right, and all is right with the world. Here you have to surrender to the benign paternalism of Shakespeare's vision. A woman alone must have a God or a dead father to guide her, but I think I can say with the particular 'authority' I have acquired by playing Helena in *All's Well That Ends Well*, that this is not the end of Shakespeare's message on the subject. It is the application of this guidance that matters.

Helena also receives a legacy from her dead father in the form of a precious medical remedy with which she manages to cure the King of France of a terminal disease. Her father has given her the wherewithal, but it takes her own particular force of character to recognise and grab the right moment to apply it. She cannot know what will come of it but she intuits that:

> There's something in't,
> More than my father's skill...
>   that his good receipt
> Shall for my legacy be sanctified
> By the luckiest stars in heaven.

But she also realises that we have to help the stars along:

> Our remedies oft in ourselves do lie,
> Which we ascribe to heaven: the fated sky
> Gives us free scope, only doth backward pull
> Our slow designs when we ourselves are dull.

Her hunch proves well founded. In both *All's Well* and *The Merchant of Venice*, the match is made fairly early in the story and the heroine needs the journey of the play to teach her some hard truths about the man of her choice.

Portia has another paternal mentor in her cousin Doctor Bellario, who instructs her in the law which she applies in the courtroom, and it is her (sometimes questionable) interpretation of that law that launches her as a rounded individual.

Portia's beautiful speech in Act III, Scene 2, where she offers everything she has up to Bassanio, '*her lord, her governor, her king'*, is not nearly so hard for an actress to get behind as the comparable speech of Kate to Petruchio at the end of *The Taming of the Shrew*. After all, Kate's is her final word on the matter, spoken in the final scene, so the speech appears to be the message Shakespeare intended the audience to go out with.

Portia's similar speech comes far earlier in the play, and it is the expression of a woman brimming with love of life and generosity who for years has had nowhere to put it. She has had everything money can buy, and none of that has brought her happiness. She has been mistress of her world, and now, riding on a wave of sexual longing and love, she surrenders to the novel and refreshing idea of being owned and ruled by her husband.

But how long does this last? Learning from Bassanio that he has a friend in danger of his life, the plot instantly thickens. Portia sees a chance to help, to save Antonio and thereby earn even more of Bassanio's love.

Within minutes she is taking charge of Bassanio's life, organising the wedding, packing him off to Venice with money enough to get Antonio off the hook, and she will then order her servant to go to Doctor Bellario, entrust the running of her house to Lorenzo and Jessica (to whom, incidentally, she shows no racist hostility, contrary to what has sometimes been suggested), and recruit Nerissa into the 'adventure' of disguising as lawyers. Finally she will win a court case and save Antonio's life. Hardly the achievements of a submissive wife!

For Shakespeare's audience there was an inherent rationale when a woman disguised herself as a man: she may need a job in an exclusively male court (Viola in *Twelfth Night*), or she may need to survive in a wild forest (Rosalind in *As You Like It*), or she may need an entrée into a world from which women were normally barred. In Portia's case this is the legal profession. It is worth noting here that it was more acceptable for the lowly Helena to take on the role of a female doctor precisely because of her class. Portia, being an heiress, was more socially prized and therefore more strictly confined.

Logically Portia could have sent for Doctor Bellario himself and paid him a tidy sum to fight Antonio's case, but then Shakespeare's audience would have been deprived of the comic irony of a boy playing a woman playing a boy. There is also a deeper psychologically rooted reason for her disguise which Shakespeare may or may not have intended, since it is only with the advent of women players that it could truly be revealed. This reason goes to the heart of the love triangle.

Almost immediately after winning the man of her dreams, Portia learns that Antonio loves Bassanio so much that he is willing to give his life for him. Without necessarily suspecting that any homosexual love exists between the two men, Portia is troubled and indeed at first feels competitive with Antonio to demonstrate the extent of her love: '*Since you are dear bought I will love you dear.*' (Note that Shakespeare gives a mercantile ring to the measure of her love, and this runs throughout the play.)

Suddenly Portia is reminded that her husband is a stranger, a man with a past, with an allegiance to an older man that she doesn't fully understand. It is this anxiety, I think, that prompts the idea of a disguise. As the lawyer Balthasar, she will enter the male world. She will get closer to Antonio and thereby tame her fears, or at least understand them, and she has a chance to save Antonio's life, thereby proving her 'superior' love to Bassanio. What she hadn't bargained for was meeting Shylock, and the lessons she would learn about herself, her husband, and the sullied, 'real' (i.e. male) world.

Portia has a sharp mind that has been wasted in her sheltered life in Belmont. In the courtroom she will exercise her innate abilities that we often think of as 'masculine', those of decisiveness, logic and authority. Her disguise will make these qualities acceptable for themselves, rather than as 'exceptional' in a woman. She has been thoroughly briefed by Doctor Bellario in the laws of Venice, and she can't wait to put all this to the test. She is used to commanding the world of Belmont, but this is an altogether different world.

Imagine her exhilaration as 'Balthasar' struts into the court with the arrogance of ignorance. She quickly sizes up the room, her opponent Shylock, and her 'rival' Antonio. She spots Bassanio and hopes he doesn't recognise her. Her eloquence soon starts to flow as she argues for the highest ideals in human nature in her famous speech about the quality of mercy. I used to think of this speech as the equivalent of my somehow bursting in on Ronald Reagan in the Oval Office and saying, 'Lay off Nicaragua. You'd feel so much better for it in yourself.' What she says in the Mercy speech is beautiful and true but, as it turns out, naive in the circumstances. She is humbled to learn that her idealistic silvery tongue has worked no magic on Shylock. She has no conception of his agenda.

I have read Ellen Terry and other actresses on Portia, and I talked to Peggy Ashcroft about her interpretation. This is not to copy them (if only!) or steal their ideas, but it was enlightening to discover that each actor had made slightly different choices for Portia in the trial scene. I was also reassured to find that I was at least addressing myself to familiar questions: To what extent has Portia prepared her argument? When does she go 'off book'? Does she enter the court knowing that she has an ace up her sleeve should all pleas for mercy fail, or does she invent it on the spot?

There is no right answer, only what can be sustained within the production you are in. No one else need know your decisions, and it is by holding on to your own private secret that the part becomes truly your own. You start thinking as and for Portia.

This was my plan (and for the above reasons, other actors will choose otherwise): Portia must prove beyond doubt that Shylock will carry out his bond to its logical end, i.e. Antonio's death. In seeking this proof she exceeds her brief. She is thinking on her feet. She impresses on him at the end of the famous Mercy speech that if he proceeds in his case,

> This strict court of Venice
> Must needs give sentence 'gainst the merchant there.

In other words, 'You do realise exactly what you are doing, don't you?' She tries two or three times to inspire him to be merciful. She offers him *'thrice thy money'*. Still he refuses. She has an attitude to this: a mixture of disgust, sorrow and humiliation. Now she is improvising. Why doesn't she stop then and say 'Got you!'? No. She wants further proof. (That Antonio is her rival and she wants to see him suffer is a red herring that I have heard suggested. Isn't that using a sledgehammer to crack a nut? And where is this idea of Portia's sadism borne out in any other part of the play?)

Shylock believes in the rule of law. Portia must demonstrate justice by using only the rule of law and thereby teach Shylock about mercy by playing the rules of his game. She of the quick wits seizes on a clue about Shylock's character: his insistence on the absolute letter of the law. At one point, when 'Balthasar' tells Antonio to *'Bear your bosom'*, Shylock jumps in:

> Ay, his breast!
> So says the bond, doth it not?…
> Nearest his heart, those are the very words.

And again later when Portia/Balthasar asks Shylock to have a surgeon standing by to stop Antonio's wound, Shylock asks,

> Is it so nominated in the bond?

Portia (slightly shocked) replies,

It is not so express'd: but what of that?
'Twere good you do so much for charity.

Shylock protests,

I cannot find it: 'tis not in the bond.

Suddenly Portia switches the focus on to Antonio and asks him to speak. This buys her time to scrutinise the bond. She has suddenly had a brainwave, unlooked-for and unplanned. 'Okay, Shylock, if you're going to nitpick about the letter of the law, I'll play that game too.' She builds Shylock up to expect his moment of triumph. He is almost whetting his knife... Then, with the most perfect theatrical timing, Portia suddenly stops him with:

Tarry a little; there is something else.

Unison intake of breath from the courtroom. Portia is chancing her luck:

Prepare thee to cut off the flesh.
Shed thou no blood, nor cut thou less nor more
But just a pound of flesh: if thou cut'st more
Or less than a just pound, be it but so much
As makes it light or heavy in the substance,
Or the division of the twentieth part
Of one poor scruple, nay, if the scale do turn
But in the estimation of a hair,
Thou diest and all thy goods are confiscate.

The letter of the law made no mention of blood and everyone knows it will be impossible for Shylock to cut just one pound of flesh from Antonio's body without spilling a drop of his blood. For Portia and the actress playing her, it is a thrilling but disturbing moment.

The extraordinary and wonderful thing about the trial scene in particular is that *it* teaches you how to play it. I laid my plans, thought it through logically step by step, but when I came to play it I *experienced* it. I learnt things about myself, and I am sure Portia learnt similar things, and this added a whole other dimension that Shakespeare never envisaged since he never expected a woman to bring her experience of life to bear in the playing of it. Portia triumphs, and Shakespeare's audience would have delighted in the cleverness of the boy. My own woman's sensibilities in going through the trial scene picked up the horror Portia must have felt on first entering this hate-filled arena, the pain she must have felt on hearing Bassanio say to Antonio that

> Life itself, my wife, and all the world,
> Are not with me esteem'd above thy life,

and, more strange than all of these, I felt the disconcerting thrill of power.

Few acting roles for women let loose this opportunity to command, to match the great weight of Shylock and control the rhythm, timing, thoughts and feelings of audience and courtroom alike. I learnt that I could do it. I enjoyed it, felt ashamed of it, felt jealous of my male counterparts that they so often get a go at it. Like Portia I had a moment's insight into what it was to be a man. At the end of this scene, I played her troubled by her own victory, unhappy at her part in upholding the law made by Venetian men against an alien, and disturbed by the suffering of Shylock when she hears him say,

> You take my life
> When you do take the means whereby I live.

This lack of complacency pays dividends when entering the final act, where Portia and Nerissa put Bassanio and Gratiano through a mock trial for having given away their betrothal rings. Portia now sees that: '*So shines a good deed in a naughty world*', and we feel her to be authorised now to judge Bassanio.

In the little interlude just after the trial (Act IV, Scene 1), we highlighted the moment at which Portia intuits that there is a possible sexual relationship between Antonio and

Bassanio. As a boy, I openly flirted with Bassanio in order to get him to part with his ring. Protesting that he promised his wife never to part with it, Bassanio resisted 'Balthasar' but was obviously turned on by him/her, much to his confusion. Then, minutes later, Gratiano comes running up to Portia/Balthasar and gives her the ring that Bassanio has now surrendered. Portia can only guess that Antonio has persuaded him to change his mind.

It is a bitter pill for her to swallow. Knowing all this, it is essential that Portia take Bassanio through the consequences of his act to finally realise that the boy and the woman are one and the same. She does this in Act V, in a delightfully funny and ultimately merciful way, though not without an underlying seriousness, nor without the sad acknowledgement that it is finally Antonio's word that releases Bassanio into heterosexual love.

Portia is by no means perfect, but she has a loving spirit and a capacity to learn and understand life that earns her the right to carry the moral torch at the end of the play. If she never moved from Belmont why would we listen to her, to a woman who hasn't glimpsed the real world nor ever dirtied her hands? We need to respect Portia even when we don't yet particularly like her.

The fun of the part is to show her transition not only from girl to boy and back, but from spoilt little rich girl to a somewhat sobered, wise and generous wife. It is the lessons she learns that make her tolerable, and by Act V we feel for the hurt love she has experienced and we want a bit of payback for Bassanio, before the forgiveness and the moving on to what we hope will be a fairly balanced marriage. All this is achieved in a lighthearted bitter-sweet manner which, for me, more than justifies the existence of the final act—which Henry Irving cut because Shylock's part was over!

Viola/Cesario

Twelfth Night also deals with the transition of love from the homosexual to the heterosexual via an androgynous catalyst; this time Viola/Cesario. For me, *Twelfth Night* is the play in which Shakespeare perfects his gender-mixing theme and puts it at the very heart of the plot. *Twelfth Night* plays with pain and dresses it as comedy. We laugh, cry and wince at the madness of love and feel the aching pleasure of it.

The disguise

In my ongoing quest to vary the 'boys', I make notes about the differences between Portia and Viola. Portia is in charge, knows how to act, has a legal brain, knew she had these all along and was *'aweary of this great world'* that wouldn't let her use them. She is also a convincing actor. Viola, on the other hand, is catapulted unwillingly into her disguise by her extreme circumstances, and that disguise is so see-through that all at Orsino's court take a jibe at it. Feste the clown has a few ambiguous comments about 'him' and even Malvolio has noticed that

> He is very well-favoured and he speaks very shrewishly.

Call me pedantic, but I wanted to find a psychologically believable reason for Viola's disguise over and above a pretext for comedy and confusion. I am sure this is a modern-day approach that the boy players of Shakespeare's day eschewed. Shakespeare has done all the thinking work for you, so why not just get on with speaking the lines, mimicking the emotions and expertly serving up the gags, as I suspect the boy players did? Blame it on the cinema, or Method Acting, or simply on the natural evolution of taste, but modern audiences set up more barriers to the suspension of disbelief than was true in Shakespeare's day.

It has been suggested to me that Viola has her eye on the main chance, noting Orsino's bachelor status in the first scene, and entering his service with a view to trapping him into marriage. (Does anyone think that clearly when they've just escaped death and believe their brother has drowned?)

Theories can sound attractive, but when you come to play the part they often just don't stand up from the inside. It has also been suggested that Viola uses her wiles to make Olivia fall in love with her so she can string out her job as messenger and not lose her place in Orsino's court. It sounds a bit flimsy to me. My answer to all this is that Viola soliloquises, and there is no example in the canon of a character lying to the audience in a soliloquy. Viola's soliloquies are full of confusion and 'what the hell is going on?' If she harboured any of the above schemes I think the audience would be let in on them.

So this is my thinking: 'Here I am shipwrecked, a lone virgin, having lost my twin brother. What would Daddy have done?' (Again the endorsement of the dead father.) 'He'd have gone straight to the top man...'

—Who governs here?...

—Orsino? I have heard my father name him.

He was a bachelor then.

Even better, Daddy actually knew of this man. 'Daddy' died when I, Viola, was thirteen, and if Orsino was remarkable for being a bachelor then, it could argue for an older Orsino who is more acquainted with wars than women. Or, if Orsino is younger, it might suggest that Daddy had mentioned his name in front of Viola, thinking that, one day, when they were both older, they would make a good match. Both scenarios are plausible but we opted for the former.

'If Orsino is a bachelor,' thinks Viola, 'I can't seek asylum in his household as an unchaperoned virgin...

What's that? He's in love with Olivia? Who's she?'

'*A virtuous maid, the daughter of a Count / That died some twelve-month since.*' He left her in the care of her brother '*who shortly also died*'.

'What a coincidence! We two should get along famously! I'll go and serve her till something shows up... But she might not let anyone enter her household?... She's a recluse? Ah well then, there's nothing for it. I'll have to go to the Duke's house, but for reasons of propriety I'll dress as a boy and serve in his household.'

All perfectly logical, I thought, but somehow when I started rehearsing, it seemed too rational and too schematic for someone as traumatised as Viola is at that point, and I eventually found a more instinctive, more unconscious motive.

Here is my potted psychology: Sebastian is Viola's twin. They were both orphaned at thirteen. Together they make a whole. They are yin and yang. If Sebastian (yin) is drowned, Viola (yang) needs to become that yin in order to fill the gap that the loss of her other half has made and to complete the male/female circuit within herself.

Viola ditches her old identity and invents Cesario (and in fact her real name is never mentioned in the play until Sebastian greets her in the last scene, and her identity is restored). There is also the thought that somehow by *becoming* her brother he is no longer dead. So her disguise is her hope. It is also the trigger for a whole set of new problems for her.

The go-between

Viola/Cesario is in more than one sense the go-between. Not only is she the messenger who can pass freely between the female-centred household of Olivia and the exclusively male court of Orsino, but she also crosses fluidly over the lines between girlhood, boyhood, youth and maturity. Malvolio describes him/her as:

> Not yet old enough for a man, nor young enough for a
> boy; as a squash is before 'tis a peascod, or a codling when
> 'tis almost an apple.

Viola embodies the cusp between all these states. Both Olivia
and Orsino have created a sort of ghetto around themselves
and only Feste and 'Cesario' can move between the two.
Viola becomes subjectively involved in both places, and both
are transformed by her presence. She achieves all this by
default. She does not feel her instrumentality in the trans-
formation. Fate is playing with her as much as with anyone
else. She has none of Portia's proactive confidence.

On her first assignment to Olivia, Viola overplays the part
and pushes the bravado a bit too far, out of nervousness. But
the enmeshing of two sexual personae in the physical presence of Cesario works on Olivia, who has *'abjured the
company / And sight of men'* and will only admit a creature
that is *'in standing water between boy and man'*.

It also works on the all-male household of Orsino, who
finds *'I have unclasp'd / To thee the book, even of my secret
soul'*, and who, when describing Cesario, says *'all is sembla-
tive a woman's part'*.

When playing Viola I never forget I am a woman, just as
she can't because she is so in love with a man who thinks
she's a boy. This is a constant, painful reminder for her, and
her femininity risks seeping out all over the place to betray
her. There is also a sense in which she *wants* to be unmasked.
She seems to be flying deliberately close to the wind when
she tells Orsino that

> My father had a daughter loved a man,
> As it might be, perhaps, were I a woman,
> I should your lordship.

—and then smilingly describes that daughter as sitting like

> Patience on a monument,
> Smiling at grief.

Even more nervy, she looks Orsino in the eye tempting him with the riddle,

> I am all the daughters of my father's house,
> And all the brothers too,

then the ambiguous

> and yet I know not.

which I played in various ways, but lately I have been play-ing it as 'I know not whether I am the only brother, because I still hope that my real brother is alive.' Then, having boldly offered the Duke a glimpse into my heart, I recover man-to-man, servant-to-master decorum with

> Sir, shall I to this lady?

In Olivia's presence, Viola transforms from the subservient adorer to unwitting adoree. The scenes with Olivia are like perfect musical duets between a flute and a clarinet (or per-haps a violin and a viola?). Hovering over the scenes is the thought of a girlie sisterhood that would unite the two orphans mourning their brothers' deaths. (It is not for noth-ing that their names are almost anagrams.) With Olivia, Viola feels more at ease acting out her masculine side than when she is inhibited by the presence of Orsino. She quickly takes over the initiative of the scene from the haughty Olivia, who in her turn backs down to become a babbling, lovelorn fool. The turning point seems to be when Viola's own passion for Orsino bursts out with:

> If I did love you in my master's flame,
> With such a suffering, such a deadly life,
> In your denial I would find no sense;
> I would not understand it.

Something in that passion prompts Olivia to ask,

> Why, what would you?

Her interest has switched from the message to the messenger.

Unaware of this, Viola relishes the question and acts out the wooing she would do if only she were free, in her famous 'willow cabin' speech. Viola is released into a transport of beautiful invention which surprises even herself, and Olivia is well and truly smitten.

Viola soon becomes aware of what has happened when Malvolio delivers Olivia's message with the ring. Her immediate response is:

> I left no ring with her: what means this lady?

but she hits on the truth in the very next line:

> Fortune forbid my outside have not charm'd her!

—which is a pretty speedy conclusion and indicates that something odd in Olivia's look or behaviour had already set up the thought in Viola's unconscious mind. After all, she knows the signs of a woman in love.

Never in the play does Shakespeare give Viola a jealous thought or word about Olivia, and now, as it becomes clearer and clearer to her that Olivia is in love with the non-existent Cesario, she expresses nothing but sisterly pity. It is a wonderful soliloquy that brings her step by step into line with the audience's understanding. But she is in the play, and they are not. They cannot help her.

> O time! thou must untangle this, not I;
> It is too hard a knot for me to untie!

From this point on, Viola is caught in the absurd situation of having to keep visiting Olivia for both Orsino's and Olivia's own reasons and all very much against her own will. She has now got personal proof that Olivia will never love Orsino, and she needs to tell Olivia not to waste her time on 'Cesario'. She is becoming impatient with Orsino. 'Leave off that hopeless case and see the love here under your very nose!' She also has to be cruel to Olivia and reject her while understanding the pain of rejection. Does this make her understand better how Olivia can reject Orsino? Her speech wraps up her true identity in another riddling hint:

> I have one heart, one bosom and one truth,
> And that no woman has; nor never none
> Shall mistress be of it, save I alone.

She wants to be discovered and released from this farce.

What's so funny?

To Elizabethans there was an almost inexhaustible joke built into the situation of a boy playing a girl playing a boy that we modern audiences have to go without. In its place we have an altogether new joke, unintended by Shakespeare; that of a girl playing a boy playing a girl dressed as a boy. Maybe it is not such a good 'joke'. Some say that women are not as funny as men. I look around me in a time of burgeoning female comic talent and I doubt this. Maybe it has been a case of audiences finding it hard to laugh at women.

Portia and Viola are allowed to make lewd quips, protected as they are by their male disguise. The boy players of Shakespeare's day were also protected by the fact of their masculinity, so that many female characters can be quite blue in their language with one another (Princess Katherine and her maid Alice, or Doll Tearsheet and Mistress Quickly, to name a couple of examples). It also rather depends on their social position as to whom they can share these jokes with. Portia makes them with Nerissa, never Bassanio. Viola's sole confidantes are in the audience, and she tells only them that

> A little thing would
> Make me tell them how much I lack of a man.

I wonder whether Shakespeare would have written that joke if a woman had played the part.

I don't think that Viola is a naturally comic role. In the reviews in Stratford someone commented that I played the first scene too like a tragedy, but consider her situation:

Viola is shipwrecked, an orphan in a foreign land where no one knows her, and she believes her twin brother and only relative has been drowned. She then falls in love with a man who thinks she's a boy, and who is infatuated with another woman, and is sent to woo that rival on behalf of the man she loves. Olivia then falls in love with her boy disguise. The audience revels in these complications. Viola does not. Viola isn't Rosalind, loved and in love, delighting in the freedom of her disguise and knowing she can drop it at any time (in the forest at least).

Viola triggers a lot of comedy but does not crack a lot of jokes. It seems to me that the comedy in *Twelfth Night* works along a spectrum of self-knowledge with the most self-deceived at one end (Malvolio, Aguecheek), whose idiocy we laugh *at*, and at the other, the most self-aware, Viola (the only character on stage aware of her real identity), whose wit we laugh *with*. We laugh *at* Orsino, who is blinded by love, and at Olivia, who is blind to her vanity in mourning, and at both of them, who are blind to the fact that Cesario is a girl. Sebastian, the 'drowned' brother, walks into a chaos he cannot make head or tail of, and we laugh at his confusion. We wryly laugh *with* Feste, the all-knowing fool, and with Maria, the traditional cunning maid, and we uncomfortably laugh with Belch, who thinks he knows it all and revels in exploiting other people's weakness.

Although Viola is the most knowing in one way, she is on totally unfamiliar ground (physically and emotionally), and this is a source of comedy for the all-knowing audience.

So I do get into the comedy eventually, and I have changed the first scene a bit for the London run (and got better reviews!). There is so much fun in the scenes with Olivia, but any wit in the scenes with Orsino remains a wistful wit, laden with Viola's desperate trapped love. The audience smiles rather than laughs at her.

Then there is the physical comedy of the sword fight between the terrified Cesario and the cowardly Aguecheek (which was enhanced for me by the instability of David Bradley/Aguecheek's wig), at the end of which Viola detects a glint of hope that Sebastian may be alive. From this point on, Shakespeare seems to let go of Viola's pain. The audience knows that Sebastian is en route to meeting up with her, that a happy ending is in sight, and all will be resolved. Or will it?

In the final scene there are some untied-up ends that leave a residue of unease. Malvolio's humiliation seems unwarranted (and unfunny) to a modern audience, and I never can quite get what that is all about—something to do with puritans versus *'cakes and ale'* guzzlers? The Roundhead-versus-Cavalier schism that was already building up to the Civil War forty years down the road? What was Malvolio's terrible sin? Self-deception, pomposity and narrow-mindedness don't seem to deserve being locked in a dark room and driven mad, so that leaves a bit of a stain on the evening. And then there is poor Aguecheek with his broken pate dealing with the harsh rejection of his 'friend' and champion Sir Toby. And what about Orsino and Viola?

In the last scene of the play, I still find it unspeakably hard to ditch the logic I have painstakingly built up and suddenly play a Viola who is so thick she doesn't twig that Sebastian is alive and the cause of everyone's confusion. After all she was quick enough on the uptake at the end of Act III, Scene 4. When she hears Antonio tell her, *'Thou hast, Sebastian, done good feature shame'*, her immediate reaction as Antonio is led off under arrest is: *'O, prove true, / That I, dear brother, be now ta'en for you!'*

She has almost pieced it together with:

> He named Sebastian: I my brother know
> Yet living in my glass; even such and so
> In favour was my brother…
> For him I imitate: O, if it prove,
> Tempests are kind and salt waves fresh in love,

but for the sake of his comic dénouement in Act V, Shake-speare changes Viola into a dumb watcher of a ping-pong match. After my initial resistance, I now willingly surrender to the rules of the comedy game, although there is still a slight insecurity in Viola over Orsino's love. We will be wonderful pals and even maybe have great sex, but will he still dream of Olivia?

At the start of their respective stories, Bassanio and Orsino have this in common: they put women on a pedestal. Their love is idealistic and immature, and they have no real knowledge of the women they adore. On the other hand they experience a strong connection with a boy (in Bassanio's case very fleetingly), and both are disturbed by this attraction they feel. But all is well in the end, when that boy proves to be a woman. That woman has now gained stature in the man's eyes by dint of having been enabled by their disguise to show their 'male' attributes of daring action, forthrightness and worldly knowledge. They have shown themselves to be one of the lads. Shakespeare could have his fun and then restore convention at the end, to please and appease the crowd.

A feminist postscript

The hardest thing to get behind in Viola is that she trusts that Time will and must sort everything out. She happens to be proved right, but not before various pates have been broken and she herself has volunteered to be sacrificed.

One textual change I have made is in Viola's '*I left no ring with her*' speech, where she talks of impressionable women with their 'waxen hearts'. Instead of

> Alas, our frailty is the cause, not we!
> For such as we are made of, such we be,

I have substituted '*For such as we are made, if such we be*'. One vowel change makes quite a big difference to me, and I have read this version in one or two editions.

A feminist actor sometimes has to find clues and take chances to express her character in the most positive light possible without damaging the whole truth of the piece. 'Why do I use this word and not that?' 'Why do I agree to betray so and so?' 'Why do I allow myself to be treated this way without protest?' One hopes that honest questioning will lead to honest answers. We can and must try to be as open as possible to new experiences, to be as unprejudiced as possible and willing to learn from other people, but at the end of the day we test everything up against our own truth.

I experience myself as a subjective whole, not as defined by men, or as being that which men are not. I see the women in Shakespeare's plays as whole people, and, when 'inhabiting', I imagine that the constraints I feel as to what I am 'allowed' to do or say are equally frustrating to me as they were to the women of the day.

I have thought of Shakespeare as a fixed and finite person, just as we fix our parents' identities and lock them into some unchanging attitude or role. Then I remind myself that he wrote as a young man and a middle-aged man, and that he was thrashing out ideas throughout his life and changing his mind as we all do. The plays are each written at a different point in his own life story, and his own fluid sexuality weaves through so many of them.

If I glance at the chronological order of his plays, his first really sympathetic female portrayal is Juliet. From *Romeo and Juliet* till 1600 he writes some fabulous women's roles: Constance in *King John*, Margaret of Anjou in *Henry VI*, Beatrice in *Much Ado*, Portia in *The Merchant*, and Helena in the *Dream*. Then suddenly we get Hamlet and his bitter misogyny, and around the same time he writes *Twelfth Night* almost to redress the balance. In the Sonnets he seems to be working through the pain of lost, forbidden or unrequited love, and if in *Hamlet* he expresses the dark side of these themes, *Twelfth Night* seems to bring them out into the comic light.

Twelfth Night is his most perfectly balanced play. He is kind to all the characters except Malvolio—and even he gets his moment of pity at the end.

IMOGEN
Peeling Back the Layers

As Imogen
Cymbeline, Royal Shakespeare Company, 1987

I wrote this piece for Volume 3 of Players *of* Shakespeare (*Cambridge University Press, 1993*) *at the invitation of the Shakespeare Institute in Stratford, who had initiated and developed a connection between the actors currently playing at the theatre and their academic students. Our production of* Cymbeline *in the RSC's 1987–8 season was directed by Bill Alexander. We started off at The Other Place (the original building, which was little more than a tin shack and a thrillingly close-up venue for actors and audience alike).*

Princess/Wife

I once heard a joke about an actor in *King Lear* being asked what the play was about; he replied, 'Oh, it's about this doctor who has to tend a sick demented old man who thinks he's King of Britain.' He, of course, was playing the doctor. From the moment we are invited to play a part, a mental process gets under way, intended to bridge the gap between 'me' and the character. Subjectivity begins to set in, and for a while our character becomes the centre of our universe. Consequently there is a sense in which for me *Cymbeline* is about Imogen. As work is beginning, however, we fight to keep our objectivity, to keep doors open, to allow the not-yet-too-subjective insights of fellow actors to throw light on the whole play and our part in it, because, of course, the meaning of the play is revealed through all the characters.

In the early stages of rehearsal, we focused on identifying the main themes of *Cymbeline*. We had ambitious talks about politics and world peace, animated discussions about love and sexual jealousy, and so on. Before I became too obsessed with Imogen, I hoped to root my work firmly in the common ground discovered with the company. If I succeeded, then anything I now say about the journey of Imogen might help uncover more of the meaning of the play.

Imogen is a coveted role. It is her range that chiefly appeals. In one evening an actress can play a bit of Desdemona, Juliet, Cordelia, Lady Anne, Rosalind and Cleopatra. In reading up about Imogen, I came across many descriptive adjectives: 'divine', 'enchanting', 'virtuous', all of which are observations and judgments not terribly helpful to the player.

As I see it, my preparatory task is to read and read and read the text and not make too many decisions about the character. I let the rhythm of her words work on me. I hoped this would help me retrace Shakespeare's steps from the word, to the thought, to the motivation, to the heart of Imogen. I must understand her choices, temporarily inhabit the mind that makes them, say her words and perform her actions, and hope thereby to make her 'live'. In performance, I will inevitably expose her to the audience's judgment, but I myself must approach her without prejudice. Luckily, *Cymbeline* not being a much-performed play, Imogen is not well known.

What are the given facts? She is the only daughter of the King of Britain. Her two brothers were stolen in infancy. Her mother is dead. Her father has remarried a scheming woman who plans to marry off her son Cloten to Imogen, now the sole heir to the British crown. Imogen has in fact secretly married Posthumus, an orphan whom her father adopted at birth and reared as Imogen's childhood companion. The opening scene of the play establishes what at court is commonly thought of all these people. Imogen and Posthumus are goodies, and reflect one another's worth:

> To his mistress...
> ...her own price
> Proclaims how she esteem'd him; and his virtue
> By her election may be truly read
> What kind of man he is.

Cloten and the Queen are baddies, and King Cymbeline is a potential goody who has lost his way.

Imogen is no ordinary obedient virgin, though she is assumed by everyone at court to be both. The audience knows that Imogen is secretly married.

We learn from Posthumus (Act II, Scene 5) that

> Me of my lawful pleasure she restrain'd,
> And pray'd me oft forbearance.

We decided that the marriage was consummated, but she sometimes had a headache.

The '*pudency so rosy*' that Posthumus describes when she occasionally turns him down could demonstrate an acceptably modest appetite or, more likely, a practical mind. Imogen must not get pregnant and blow their cover prematurely.

So Imogen has dared go against her father's wishes by marrying Posthumus, which is tantamount to rebelling against her King. I decided she had married impulsively with no great plan in mind, but somehow was instinctively defending herself with a *fait accompli* in order to put a stop to the projected marriage with Cloten. When the shit finally hits the fan she'll think again.

The clue to this characteristic impetuosity I found in her later lines (Act III, Scene 2):

I see before me, man; nor here, nor here,
Nor what ensues.

She seems to have a defiantly independent version of what is right and she sticks to it. Call it integrity or call it arrogance, her strength and her chief fault are two sides of the same coin. She starts off the play with a strong sense of her own importance, both as lawful wife to Posthumus and as Princess of Britain. Her sense of self is intricately bound up in those two titles, and the events of the play unsettle her faith in both.

At the beginning of her story I discovered a quality in Imogen that I could never clearly describe. It was a kind of self-dramatisation. It is as though in order to bear her misery, she casts herself in a noble role, and, in playing that to the hilt, she cannot be seen to give in or let herself down. She starts by choosing her own roles, but as the play goes on, fate and other people will force her into many disguises. These have a narrative justification and function, but on a deeper level they have the quality of metamorphoses. They are in some way like a series of small deaths and rebirths in another form, and involve giving up some outer trapping of her identity the better to find her true self.

Through all these outward changes she retains the core of her Imogen-ness. I hoped that if I didn't define that Imogen-ness in advance but played each situation and role for what it was, the Imogen-ness would take care of itself. It would reveal itself not in spite of, but because of, the disguise. I found it helpful to signpost her journey in terms of these metamorphoses, which could be labelled: Princess to Princess-Wife/Princess-Wife to Rebel/Rebel to Franklin's Housewife/Franklin's Housewife to Boy/Boy to Roman Page/Roman Page to Princess-Wife.

First Metamorphosis: Princess-Wife to Rebel

> A wedded lady, that hath her husband banish'd.

Cymbeline has discovered that Imogen and Posthumus are married. Posthumus is banished, and Imogen is under house-arrest. What with Posthumus's banishment, her father's rejection, Cloten's assaults, and the scheming of the Queen, she has a lot to cope with. In Act I, Scene 1, she yearns to be a 'neat-herd's daughter', but, sensible of her royal status, she draws strength from a knowledge that she isn't just anyone going through a personal tragedy, but that there are subjects out there relying on her to survive with all the values of the Old Britain intact.

This sureness of her role gives her the courage to tell her father,

> I am senseless of your wrath.

He is like the *'tyrannous breathing of the north'* that *'shakes all our buds from growing'*.

Both David Bradley (playing Cymbeline) and I wanted to show that theirs was the rage that comes from betrayal of what had been great love between them. This endows Cymbeline with the humanity he will need in the final scene and helps our reconciliation at the end. This was not an intellectual imposition on our part but arose from both of our instinctive responses to the scene as soon as we put it on its feet. There seemed to be something so immediate and intimate in the confrontation between them; a suggested matching of temperaments. It reminded me of other father/daughter conflicts—Cordelia and Lear, Juliet and Capulet—that, despite the hostility of the moment, show quite uncluttered channels of communication, open to great love as well as great antagonism.

Apart from the loyal Pisanio, whom Posthumus has left her as a kind of parting gift, Imogen has no ally. For most of the run in Stratford we emphasised the friendship between

Pisanio and Imogen. Actors are often both tactile and insecure (maybe the former because of the latter), so I found
myself accompanying every 'good Pisanio' and 'true Pisanio'
with a clutch of Jim Hooper's wrist or an arm round his
shoulder. Wrong: he is a servant and she a princess, and
when we came to re-rehearse the play for Newcastle, Bill
Alexander encouraged me to be more regally distant with
Pisanio. Stressing this gulf in status pays off later when Imogen must somehow believe Pisanio capable of murdering
Posthumus. She has not been reared in an atmosphere of
great trust, if Belarius's descriptions of the court are accurate, but because of Pisanio's connection to Posthumus she
trusts him with all her plans.

Our production was simply staged at The Other Place,
with the audience sitting very close to the action, in a rough
circle of random wooden chairs. The first scene between
Pisanio and Imogen (Act I, Scene 3) took place in what we
imagined to be almost a hidey-hole, lit only by one candle,
which seemed to symbolise the memory of Posthumus that
we were conspiratorially keeping alive. We could talk almost
in a whisper. Cries of 'Imogen' from the Queen down a corridor somewhere added to the dangerous atmosphere.

Imogen feels almost competitive with Pisanio in her devo-
tion to Posthumus. As Pisanio describes watching
Posthumus's departure from the shore, Imogen interrupts
and tops him every time:

Thou shouldst have made him
As little as a crow…

I would have broke mine eye-strings…
Nay, follow'd him, till he had melted from
The smallness of a gnat to air, and then
Have turn'd mine eye and wept.

Because she and Posthumus have been brought up together,
I imagine their relationship not unlike that of Cathy and
Heathcliff. Childhood companions, twin souls sharing

secrets, brother and sister suddenly become man and wife. Sexual knowledge opens the Pandora's box of jealousy, fear of loss, mistrust and ignorance of the opposite sex. They are parted at a vulnerable stage in their development together. Sex has the power to make them strangers to one another, and it is that power that Iachimo exploits when he meets the exiled Posthumus in Rome.

Imogen betrays early on her suspicions of the '*shes of Italy*' (of course in this case it is not just her mistrust of other women, but of Italy in general she is showing) and on parting with Posthumus she (again slightly self-dramatisingly) suggests that Posthumus might

> woo another wife
> When Imogen is dead.

One of the play's themes is '*too ready hearing*'. Belarius tells how, with little resistance, Cymbeline believed him to be '*confederate with the Romans*' through '*two villains, whose false oaths prevail'd / Before my perfect honour*'.

Posthumus (admittedly with quite tangible 'proof' contrived by Iachimo) believes Imogen to be unfaithful, and Imogen succumbs to Iachimo's suggestions of Posthumus's infidelity with what I found in the playing to be disconcerting speed. She soon realises what she's done and blames herself with:

> I do condemn mine ears that have
> So long attended thee,

and, feeling guilty at her momentary lapse of faith, she proceeds to overcompensate Iachimo with her trust, to the point where the next morning, missing her bracelet, and through all the trials that follow, she never once suspects him.

I found Act I, Scene 6, when Iachimo first visits Imogen, one of the most exciting to play. Interacting with Donald Sumpter as Iachimo, the balance of the scene minutely and importantly altered every night. I had to negotiate subtly, delicately, how much to believe when, and how quickly. Both of us enjoy being unpredictable, but there are rules even to unpredictability. One has to guard against being different for its own sake and thereby destroying the credibility for one's fellow actor.

For instance, if Don were to make Iachimo too smarmy, with Imogen's already strong prejudice against Italians would she not see through him too early on? Likewise I had to give Don/Iachimo just the right ambiguity on '*How should I be revenged?*' for him to be able to interpret it as a possible lead for his lascivious suggestion. I had to *mean* 'What would you know?... You cannot understand the enormity of this betrayal... revenge is so inappropriate', but say the line in such a way that Iachimo would be able to hear it as 'I'm at a loss to think of a suitable revenge to match this crime. Have you any ideas?'

On nights when Don/Iachimo exaggerated his account of Posthumus, the Briton reveller, creasing up at the sighing French lover—crying:

> O can my sides hold, to think that man, who knows...
> what woman is... will his free hours languish for assured
> bondage?

—I would deliver my line: '*Will my lord say so?*' in an 'Oh yeah?' kind of way. If Don played it more delicately, I'd say it with a shadow crossing my face, but an attempt at light-heartedness in my voice.

In playing Imogen in most of her other scenes, I had the sensation of driving through like a steamroller, raging at her father, overriding Pisanio, letting off volleys of insults at Cloten and the Queen. There was an element of the boxing-ring as I entered the horseshoe-shaped arena at The Other Place, or later The Pit in the Barbican, for a two-hander, head-on contest with Cloten or the King and usually come off best, if only verbally. Here with Iachimo, on the other hand, Imogen is off-footed from the start. She begins with

57

outrage at the intrusion of a stranger, and, instantly, on learning that he comes from Italy and from Posthumus, she is thrown into the opposite mood of ecstatic excitement. '*Change you, madam?*' is Iachimo's knowing understatement and Shakespeare's stage direction, all in one.

This volatility of Imogen's mood where Posthumus is concerned is the key both to her credulity and her over-quick forgiveness of Iachimo. From this point, the unconditional warmth and charm she extends to Iachimo as a fellow adorer of Posthumus is misinterpreted by Iachimo.

As in *The Winter's Tale* and *Othello*, a woman showing open friendship for a man other than her spouse is misunderstood by a misogynist onlooker or a frightened husband through his ignorance of the complex range of a woman's feelings.

Iachimo can undermine Imogen's and Posthumus's faith in one another by the same means that Iago can manipulate Othello. The thing you most prize you most fear losing. Living with that fear, in a world where propaganda perpetuates suspicion between the sexes, can become so unbearable that you break under the strain. You begin to want to believe the worst, in order to alleviate the pressure. I am sure this is why Posthumus is driven to say to Iachimo in Act II, Scene 4:

> No swearing:
> If you will swear you have not done't, you lie,
> And I will kill thee if thou dost deny
> Thou'st made me cuckold.

Loss of faith in Imogen leads Posthumus to his famous diatribe against her entire gender (Act V, Scene 4). It is significant that Imogen's reaction to the same emotion earlier on, in Act III, Scene 4, is not an equivalent railing against Posthumus and all men, but an echo of the prevailing misogyny of the world, placing the blame firmly in the female camp:

> ...some jay of Italy
> Whose mother was her painting, hath betray'd him.

Our incidental score consisted of wind-chimes, suspended oil drums, the inside of a piano, stamping feet and human calls, all arranged expertly by Ilona Sekacz. It provided atmospheric percussion throughout the play. In the bedroom scene (Act II, Scene 2) a couple of delicate strokes on a wind-chime instantly conjured up a hot night cooled by a breeze and evoked (for me anyway) the cricket-singing that Iachimo speaks of.

Imogen is reading in bed. A sudden kick of an oil drum makes her jump out of her skin: '*Who's there?*' Her woman Helen enters and Imogen asks, '*What hour is it?*'

And Helen's answer, '*Almost midnight, madam*', was delivered in such a way as to suggest this is unusually late for Imogen still to be reading. When Helen settles Imogen down for a sleep and is about to blow out the candle, I played up Imogen's nervousness by sudden fitful rhythms on:

Take not away the taper, leave it burning

and

if thou canst awake by four o'th' clock, I prithee call me.

This is followed by Imogen's prayer for protection against the '*tempters of the night*', and, as if for added security, I kissed Posthumus's bracelet, so soon to be slipped from my arm by Iachimo, just as she describes herself as having done next day in Act II, Scene 3. All of this signals a certain disquiet in Imogen that could spring from a deep-down unease about her earlier behaviour with Iachimo.

Iachimo has crept into Imogen's chamber and is hovering over her sleeping form. Taking my cue from Iachimo's speech, '*one kiss! Rubies unparagon'd, / How dearly they do't*', and tempted to play on the fine line separating seeming-guilt and innocence, I returned Iachimo's kiss in my sleep. I justified the kiss by thinking of her later admission that she dreams of Posthumus every night. Neither Iachimo nor the audience are to know for sure at this point whether it's the kiss of the actual Iachimo or the dreamed-of Posthumus that she is returning so sweetly. Again the proximity of the audience in this studio production gave the scene an almost voyeuristic edge, and for this reason I found the scene to be the ultimate in passive vulnerability.

If there are hints of Imogen's unease in the bedroom scene, they grow to full-blown dread in the following scene with Cloten (Act II, Scene 2). We know she has both the guts and the wit to stick up for herself and make mincemeat of Cloten any day of the week, but this time she goes a bit too far with her insults and tips Cloten over into a maddened vengeful rage. Cloten can be dismissed as a fool, and I laughed at his '*I'll be revenged*', but it was a laugh tinged with fear of a more dangerous man beneath. The loss of her bracelet has unnerved her.

Is she possibly nagged by some unformed notion of having done something wrong? Whatever she has done doesn't deserve Posthumus's order to Pisanio to kill her.

Second Metamorphosis: The Franklin's Housewife

I am almost a man already.

At last comes a release, both for Imogen and for the actress playing her. In Act III, Scene 2, she receives a letter from Posthumus inviting her to meet him at Milford Haven. I sat on the bottom step in the aisle six inches away from the nearest member of the audience, who could read the letter over my shoulder. I didn't sit there for long. As soon as I understood that Posthumus would be arriving imminently at Milford Haven, I leapt up—'*O, for a horse with wings!*'—and almost took flight. This speech provides an all-too-rare opportunity for vein-bursting joy. The danger for me is that exhilaration runs away with me and my tongue runs away with the words—though it is important that Pisanio gets no chance to stem the tide and interrupt. To avoid detection in her escape from the palace to Milford Haven, Imogen dresses as a '*franklin's housewife*' (a franklin was a landholder of free, but not noble, birth). It is an impulsive solution intended

> for the gap
> Which we shall make in time, from our hence-going
> And our return, to excuse.

But after the events on her arrival in Wales, that return becomes out of the question. She won't go back. She speaks of '*the perturb'd court... whereunto I never purpose return*', and when Pisanio suggests, '*If you'll back to the court...*', she jumps in on him with '*No court, no father, nor no more ado...*'

Maybe subconsciously she knew from the beginning that she was initiating a final break. Here on a Welsh hillside, humbly dressed, she learns of Posthumus's intent to kill her for her supposed adultery. The news itself as good as kills her at first. She begs Pisanio to obey Posthumus's orders as without Posthumus in her heart there's no point to her life.

She doesn't believe that Posthumus actually thinks she's false. Her honour is beyond question: '*I false? Thy conscience witness.*'

As she constructs it, he has fallen for someone else and falsely accuses her just to get her out of the way. She not only confronts literal death by Pisanio's sword, but a death of faith:

> All good seeming,
> By thy revolt, O husband, shall be thought
> Put on for villainy.

But Imogen doesn't feel suicidal for long. The confrontation brings out the fight in her. At this point, things tended to get dangerous. The advantages of the small space here became disadvantages. I found it hard to contain the size of Imogen's emotions within that little wooden 'O'. I wanted to yell from the Welsh mountain tops. When Jim as Pisanio threw his sword away and when I cast Posthumus's love-letters aside, quite often they landed at the audience's feet. Both had to be retrieved during the action, and it's hard to conjure up in one's imagination the loneliness of a clearing in a wood near Milford Haven while grovelling among Hush Puppies and handbags! From this point of view things improved in the larger Pit when we transferred to London.

Until this point, Imogen has identified herself with Britain to such an extent that when Iachimo (in Act I, Scene 7) plants doubts in her mind as to Posthumus's fidelity, she says, '*My lord, I fear, has forgot Britain.*'

The word 'Britain' also encapsulates a set of values for her. Values that she has learnt from childhood and which she also sees in Posthumus. In her book, Cymbeline has also 'forgot Britain' by banishing Posthumus:

> It is your fault that I have lov'd Posthumus:
> You bred him as my play-fellow.

With those words it seems she is saying, 'You taught me my values and now you're reneging on them. It's up to me and Posthumus to carry the flag for all that is good about Britain until you come to your senses and see through that wicked Queen who has led you up the garden path.'

Now through the trauma of Act III, Scene 4, Imogen manages to extricate her belief in Posthumus from her belief in herself, and both from her belief in Britain:

> Hath Britain all the sun that shines? Day? Night?
> Are they not but in Britain? I' th' world's volume
> Our Britain seems as of it, but not in't:
> In a great pool, a swan's nest: prithee think
> There's livers out of Britain.

In that moment, the '*strain of rareness*' she had earlier rather chest-thumpingly declared in herself becomes real. She becomes larger.

Having given up her royal identity, she next gives up her sexual identity. Unlike Rosalind and Portia, Imogen does not volunteer to disguise as a boy. It is Pisanio who advises, '*You must forget to be a woman*', and unusually, in Imogen's case, maleness does not bring with it authority, but rather it means she must '*change command into obedience*', as Pisanio puts it.

She is already well along the road to forgiving Posthumus, not a little thanks to Pisanio's constancy. Pisanio's proposal is that she travel to Italy in the service of the Roman general Caius Lucius, where she can at least be near Posthumus, and who knows what might happen then? The Princess who has barely stepped outside her castle bedroom jumps at his suggestion:

> O, for such means,
> Though peril to my modesty, not death on't,
> I would adventure.

The musical movement of this scene is so clearly indicated by Shakespeare that we just had to surrender to his 'stage directions' and, provided we didn't dodge the full force of the emotions, we could then ride it out, so to speak. To begin with, each character describes how the other should be behaving:

> Wherefore breaks that sigh
> From th' inward of thee?

and

> Put thyself into a 'haviour of less fear [etc.].

Imogen says nothing after reading Posthumus's letter, and Shakespeare gives Pisanio eight lines aside to cover her silence, beginning with:

> What shall I need to draw my sword? the paper
> Hath cut her throat already.

Then Imogen's white-hot anger takes over the scene, leaving Pisanio winded and gasping, until, exhausted, she allows him to speak. He begins tentatively, and she still manages to rush in and contradict him until, after insisting that '*some Roman courtesan*' has caused Posthumus's treachery, Jim/Pisanio forgot his servant status, grabbed me by the shoulders and fairly shook me on the line '*No, on my life.*' This shocked me first into bewilderment—'*Why, good fellow, what shall I do the while?*'—then determination, rejecting all idea of returning to court, and then giving Pisanio the cue, '*I am most glad you think of other place...*'

In a quieter, more compliant, frame of mind Imogen takes on his plan. The scene ended with Pisanio handing me back Posthumus's bundle of letters and a quiet, serious '*I thank thee*' from a finally lucid Imogen.

I am baffled and disappointed that Shakespeare doesn't reward Pisanio for what I feel to be the most virtuous conduct of all. In his final acts, Shakespeare often leaves the odd end untied so I think he just forgot about Pisanio in the tangle of other plots.

I felt for Pisanio who, as a servant, risks great punishment in disobeying orders. He knows Imogen is true without needing proof. He has been ordered by his master to kill her. He refuses. He thinks on his feet and formulates a plan to save the situation. He was given the power to kill and he didn't use it. Compare his lines in Act III, Scene 2—

> If it be so to do good service, never
> Let me be counted serviceable

—with a war criminal's 'I was only carrying out orders.' Surely the woman who went against her King/father's orders when she thought him corrupt would approve of Pisanio's attitude. I felt this so strongly I even changed a line in the final scene in Act V since no one acknowledges Pisanio's role in the happy outcome of events. I addressed '*And you relieved me to see this gracious season*' to Pisanio rather than to Belarius.

Pisanio's virtue comes from his sense of honour—

How look I,
That I should seem to lack humanity
So much as this fact comes to?

—just as Iachimo's capacity for evil comes from his lack of
self-love. To a great extent we judge others according to what
we know of ourselves. Iachimo refuses to believe in love and
fidelity between Posthumus and Imogen because he feels
incapable of such feelings himself. This is why Imogen's
belief in herself is so important. It feeds her belief in others,
which involves faith and hope. To hope requires the courage
to face the risk of loss, and courage is a quality that Imogen
is constantly called on to demonstrate.

Third Metamorphosis: Boy to Housewife

Cook to honest creatures…
I'll love him as my brother.

In her new masculine disguise, determined to bear her trials
with '*a prince's courage*', Imogen is forced to reach a more
quintessential definition of herself. She has had to slough off
'Imogen' like an old skin, and underneath she finds 'Fidele',
the faithful one. In this state, Shakespeare has prepared her
to meet her brothers, who have been exiled since birth and
have been reared in the wild by the kindly Belarius. The
meeting is geographically an outrageous coincidence, but it
is spiritually timely. She is alone and ravenous in the forest
near Belarius's cave and she is very aware of the limitations
of her physical courage (Act III, Scene 6):

If mine enemy
But fear the sword like me, he'll scarcely look on't.

But she also knows her best source of strength: '*I should be
sick, / But that my resolution helps me.*'
In Act I, Scene 7, she had said

> Had I been thief-stol'n,
> As my two brothers, happy... blessed be those,
> How mean so e'er, that have their honest wills.

Now, she's testing these ideal sentiments for real, and on meeting her brothers and finding them to be '*kind creatures*', she can confirm

> what lies I have heard.
> Our courtiers say all's savage but at court;
> Experience, O, thou disprov'st report.

The costumes for this production were all drawn from stock, and within an agreed basic framework we were free to choose the clothes we felt best fitted our image of the character. My image of Imogen was something of Boudicca and something of Fuchsia in Mervyn Peake's *Gormenghast*—the smutty rebel child grown into wilful adult with amazon potential. I chose a rough, simple velvet dress to begin with, and on becoming a boy I wore a costume based on the standard 'look' of the other men: velvet jerkin, white shirt, belt, braces, and brown trousers tucked into mid-calf boots. My thick, not-too-groomed red mane (a wig) got plaited, and my gold headband was replaced by a brown one giving me a faintly Viking look. I most decidedly didn't want to wear my own short hair at this point, as that was my image for the more gamine Viola (who I was still playing in repertoire), and I needed to differentiate between them.

With her boy disguise the pressure is somehow off Imogen and off the player of Imogen. The emotional drive relaxes, and there is more opportunity for comedy and lyricism. Shakespeare even takes her to the very edge of acceptable irony with '*would... they had been my father's sons*', at which point I willingly gave in to audience titters, though my character was in earnest. I learnt to dare to give a pause after such a line—I say 'dare' because one risks a laugh-less silence and egg on the face. The pause should be just long enough to let the audience know that they can laugh—that the actor intends the joke, though the character is innocent of it—an enjoyable knife-edge to tread.

From the confrontation with Pisanio's sword (which incidentally she forgot to fear at the time) to the first meeting with the cave-dwellers—*'if you kill me for my fault, I should / Have died had I not made it'*—Imogen has felt herself dangerously close to death, and this has led her to philosophise:

> Clay and clay differs in dignity
> Whose dust is both alike

and

> falsehood is worse in kings than beggars.

Not wildly original maybe, but quite a leap for a Princess reared in a palace as heir to the throne.

In her state of 'sad-sickness' she is prompted to swallow the drug Pisanio gave her from the Queen, and we next see her lifeless form carried on by Cadwal and lain on the ground.

This is the second occasion where I had to play drugged or asleep and was able to listen to the most beautiful passages of poetry in the play. First when Iachimo breaks into Imogen's bedroom, and then when the two cave-boys speak *'Fear no more the heat of the sun'* over Imogen's 'dead' body. Incidentally, it is not only the cave-dwellers who believe Imogen is dead. Many of the audience were convinced of it too, if they happened to have nodded off when the doctor told them that his drug was harmless and capable merely of

> locking up the spirits a time
> To be more fresh, reviving.

I often heard a gasp or even a vocalised 'Oh, no!' at the point when I swallowed the drug. This is one of the advantages of being in a little-known play. Everyone knows about Juliet!

Lying there prone on the floor with my eyes closed, I tried to allow the words to inspire me, in preparation for my most difficult acting task ahead: the scene when I wake up next to a beheaded corpse that I believe is my husband's. I knew I would have to trust the inspiration of the moment, and I lay there with my eyes closed wondering, 'Will I make it? And what will come out of me this time?', and I was rarely, if ever, satisfied with the result.

The scene is a minefield of the most fundamental acting problems. First I had to try to imagine a situation way outside my experience and which I hope will remain so. Shakespeare had already imagined the reactions of a woman in such a situation, and he had given her the words to express them. I had to bring my imagination into line with his. Secondly, there are two major traps in delivering a highly charged Shakespearean soliloquy: on the one hand, there is the temptation to impose a generalised emotion, to wash the stage with genuine tears, and drown out the words that would move the audience far more effectively; and at the other extreme there is the danger that you will have no feelings at all that night and will overcompensate by overacting. The golden rule is to trust Shakespeare and allow his words and rhythms to do their work. You are an instrument through which his music should flow. All much easier said than done.

The audience is never going to share your grief because they know the corpse belongs to Cloten. They are ahead of you and are now focusing on how you/Imogen will react, how you will deal with your grief, whether you will recover, and how you will move on. In that sense it is a bit of a public acting test, and Shakespeare is not at his most helpful when he asks Imogen to weep over Posthumus's '*martial thigh*' and '*brawns of Hercules*' with only a headless stuffed dummy to help me! I'm comforted by the knowledge that both Ellen Terry and Peggy Ashcroft also found this speech fearfully difficult.

I tried to make my reactions as unpredictable as possible and deliver up just enough weeping and wailing to give the spectators a bit of fun as they watched Imogen trying to come to terms with the unacceptable from a few feet away.

Still semi-drugged, Imogen gropes about on the ground to ascertain where on earth she is. It is like the classic movie scene when the lover has stealthily crept out of the bed leaving only a dented pillow behind. When Imogen sees (as she supposes) the headless corpse of Posthumus, she begins with a wonderfully internal and naturalistic '*I hope I dream*'. Then, when she begins to process reality: '*How should this be?*'

Shakespeare often expresses the extreme with simple, monosyllabic words. The speech builds as Imogen tries to keep a grip on her sanity. She comes up with the not altogether sane idea that Pisanio is Posthumus's murderer. She converts grief into rage. Still seeing herself as the heroine of her own story or '*the madded Hecuba*' of a Greek tragedy, she rails at the gods. She has hitherto believed herself to have a special relationship with them, and that her destiny mattered to them. She feared them but she felt their protection. Now, '*murder in heaven*' has been committed and the gods have turned against her.

From such a viewpoint she can believe even Pisanio is her enemy. She covers her face with Posthumus's blood, and lies beside him united again with him. There is a feeling of 'it's us against the world' in her speech, '*that we the horrider may seem to those / That chance to find us*'.

Desperation is about to lead her to a new disguise. The woman who had railed against '*drug-damned Italy*' and the '*Romish stew*' is about to switch to the Roman side.

When I slump in tears over the 'corpse', awaiting the arrival of General Lucius, I truly feel 'thou thy acting task hast done'. I can hand over the stage to Posthumus. Again, another part of Imogen has 'died'. She has shed her royalty, her femininity, and now she will surrender her national identity.

'*I am nothing*,' she tells the general, but still she answers to the name of Fidele.

Fourth Metamorphosis: The Roman Page

I am nothing.

Having washed my face and donned my Roman jacket for my fleeting, silent appearance in the battle scene, I then joined the rest of the company to lend musical aid (the studio production having more or less eschewed visual aids) to the descent of Jupiter in Posthumus's dream. Bashing piano wires was the one point of relaxation I had in the evening, and I could listen to Nick Farrell as Posthumus repenting for having murdered Imogen—'*O Pisanio, every good servant does not all commands*'—and wishing he was dead. He had wanted Imogen dead, but confronted with the bloody cloth that proves his wish has been fulfilled, he can't bear a world without her, and his moral rigidity bends (Act V, Scene 1):

> You married ones,
> If each of you should take this course, how many
> Must murder wives much better than themselves
> For wrying but a little?

In battle he is then given the chance to kill Iachimo and doesn't. Iachimo looks death in the face and is saved. The wild brothers are at last testing their princely blood in battle, and all the characters are being prepared for Act V, Scene 5, and the unravelling of their interwoven themes.

If we had planted the right seeds, Act V worked a treat. The play's characters have to go through some almost impossible suspensions of disbelief—not recognising people two feet away, spotting rings and birthmarks they never noticed before—as for the next thirty minutes they learn what the audience already knows. In that sense the audience are like the gods and can look on with benign amusement (and often outright laughter). But in addition, if the play has worked, they will have undergone a journey alongside the players and had a mirror held up to them, just as the characters have.

Imogen looks at Posthumus, Posthumus looks at Iachimo, Cymbeline looks at Belarius and Lucius, and all see some reflection of their own errors. There is a feeling of 'Let him that is without sin cast the first stone.' We have seen good Italians and bad; good Britons and bad; good women and bad. The barriers of sex, birth and nation have been broken down. We begin to honour the bonds instead of perpetuating the divisions. Forgiveness is within our range—'*Pardon's the word to all*,' says Cymbeline. On refinding his family, Cymbeline describes himself as the '*mother to the birth of three*'. A society has been purged (admittedly with the help of the gods and the scapegoat Queen) and reborn. Glasnost is given a chance. Restored to her final role as Princess/Wife (with the help of a blow from Posthumus which provides her final reawakening), Imogen the individual recedes and merges with the whole as, in the final image of the play, we all kneel in a circle to praise the gods.

LADY MACBETH
A Portrait of a Marriage

As Lady Macbeth with Antony Sher (Macbeth)
Macbeth, Royal Shakespeare Company, 1999

In 1999, I was asked to contribute a slim book on a Shakespeare play of my choice to what was to be a series for Faber and Faber entitled Actors on Shakespeare *(edited by Colin Nicholson). As I was about to start rehearsals for* Macbeth *at the RSC, I decided to write as I rehearsed and played the part of Lady Macbeth. This is a shortened version of that book.*

The tragedy of *Macbeth* is set in motion by two people, a man and his wife. None of it would have happened if either had been acting alone. To understand the play it is necessary to anatomise the partnership that motors it.

Like Hamlet or Falstaff, Lady Macbeth is so much part of our cultural landscape that she seems actually to exist somewhere out there. Throughout the world her name is a by-word for monstrosity, the unnatural woman, the evil power behind the throne.

In the months leading up to rehearsals I read and re-read the play with as open a mind as possible and pored over other actresses' accounts of playing the part. It was both comforting and exhilarating to commune with these ghosts, to feel part of a tiny band of people who had shared this rare and particular task down the years, but in the end I felt nearer to them than to Lady Macbeth. She remained like a mountainous wave that would break over me and crush me unless I caught it and rode it.

I suspect that if you were to ask the person-in-the-street what they knew of Lady Macbeth, most who knew anything would say something like 'She's the one who persuades her husband to kill the King...' But I was finding indications in the text that Lady M does not put the idea of killing the King into her husband's head, it is already there. There is a huge but subtle difference between coercing a totally upright person to commit a crime and working on the wavering will of someone who already wants to commit that crime but fears the consequences. I was not out to clear Lady Macbeth's name, but I wanted to straighten a few facts.

Shakespeare repeatedly uses the image of planting, and it is an apt one. Macbeth and Lady Macbeth are caught at a moment of ripeness and preparedness for evil. The witches are agents of this evil, and for that reason they do not seek out Banquo, who proves less fertile soil, but Macbeth. Lady Macbeth understands her husband as well as the witches do and builds on the work they have begun. She herself never kills, but if she had let well alone, Macbeth would not have acted. That is the considerable extent of her blame.

I had already scoured the text for any insights into Lady Macbeth as an individual, separate from her husband, but except for the odd '*most kind hostess*' or '*fair and noble hostess*' from the King, no one comments on her or throws any light on her character. Nobody seems to know her. She has no confidante. Her world is confined to the castle and its servants, but it was hard for my imagination to people the place or fill it with domestic goings-on. A Lady Macbeth busying herself with the housekeeping or taking tea with a circle of friends just did not ring true. It did not ring true because Shakespeare's creation only exists within the time-frame of the play. It was as though she had visited Shakespeare's imagination fully formed, giving away no secrets, and therein lies a lot of her power.

Back to the clues in the text: Wound up and ready for action Lady Macbeth bursts on to the stage reading her husband's letter. Interestingly the first words we hear from her mouth are his words, which immediately made me feel like his mouthpiece, the agent of his thoughts.

Having read the letter she, like Macbeth, leaps to believe the witches' prophecy that he will be King.

> Glamis thou art, and Cawdor; and shalt be
> What thou art promised.

However, she believes that '*Fate and metaphysical aid*' only 'seem [my emphasis] *to have thee crown'd withal*'.

She must give Fate a helping hand.

My Dearest Partner of Greatness

Greg Doran directed our production and Antony Sher played Macbeth. By listening to Tony's soliloquies I discovered how closely Lady Macbeth and her Lord mirror one another's thoughts and language. (I would return to this again and again as the play went on, using Macbeth's speeches to help me fathom his increasingly silent partner's state of mind.) By means of these echoes of imagery between husband and wife Shakespeare subliminally suggests a twinning of minds. Note the crossover of imagery between Macbeth's soliloquy in Act I, Scene 4:

> Stars, hide your fires;
> Let not light see my black and deep desires:
> The eye wink at the hand; yet let that be,
> Which the eye fears, when it is done, to see

and Lady Macbeth's, also spoken alone in Act I, Scene 5:

> Come, thick night,
> And pall thee in the dunnest smoke of hell,

That my keen knife see not the wound it makes,
Nor heaven peep through the blanket of the dark,
To cry 'Hold, hold!'

If the eye is sentinel to the conscience and the hand is the instrument of action, then to commit evil the two must be kept apart. The disembodied hand acts on its own beyond the responsibility of its 'owner': 'I don't know what came over me, Inspector. Next thing I knew, the gun was in my hand.' The schism between thought and deed is a familiar Shakespearean theme. As Hamlet says, '*The native hue of resolution / Is sicklied o'er with the pale cast of thought.*'

Macbeth and Hamlet would have agreed on much at the beginning of the play, but while Macbeth has become a murderer by Act II, Scene 2, Hamlet remains the philosopher to the end. Hamlet's toughest resolution is expressed in terms of thoughts rather than deeds (*Hamlet*, Act IV, Scene 4):

From this time forth,
My thoughts be bloody or be nothing worth.

By contrast when Macbeth, also in Act IV, says,

from this moment
The very firstlings of my heart shall be
The firstlings of my hand,

we know he will act on his words.

How differently would things have turned out if Hamlet had been married to Lady Macbeth? This is not a frivolous question. *Macbeth* is, among other things, the portrait of a *folie à deux*. It deals with a unique and deadly chemistry between two particular individuals. If Lady M were pure demoness she could make a murderer of anyone, even Hamlet, but she isn't. The materials have to be right, and Macbeth's personality fits. She knows him like her own skin. (Incidentally, Hamlet being a woman-blamer would probably bleat that it was all Lady M's fault—something Macbeth never does.)

When husband and wife first meet on stage they have no need to spell things out. Macbeth has three lines in the scene. He has paved much of the way in his letter. Although if anyone else had intercepted it they would find nothing incriminating, to Lady Macbeth's fertile ear it reads: 'The way is clear, my dearest partner of Greatness, and I know you will know what to do.' All he has to say when he greets her is: '*My dearest love, / Duncan comes here tonight.*'

We have already been party to Lady Macbeth's extreme reaction to the same news earlier and now she can afford a calm: '*And when goes hence?*'

(There is something of a test going on here, as though she is really asking, 'And is he going to leave here alive, do you think? If not, what are you going to do about it?')

He replies,

> Tomorrow, as he purposes.

So far, so innocent, if the room were bugged. But why add '*as he purposes*'? A simple 'Tomorrow' would have done. In the husband-and-wife telepathy this added phrase means 'at least that is what *he* thinks', and that is enough of a cue for Lady Macbeth to pounce in with '*O, never / Shall sun that morrow see!*'

Shakespeare then builds two beats of silence into the five-beat line, during which... what? It is a truly pregnant pause. Husband and wife search one another's faces, and hold their breath in shock. The thoughts they had dared think alone are now brought literally face to face. It is the moment. The time is right and what has hitherto been safe fantasy is in danger of happening. Both are terrified, but she is better at covering it up. Her next words dictate something of how the actor must play Macbeth in that moment.

> Your face, my thane, is as a book, where men
> May read strange matters.

This has a doubly ironic ring if the audience remembers King Duncan's observation in the previous scene, that '*There's no art / To find the mind's construction in the face*', seconds before a seemingly loyal Macbeth enters and kneels at his feet. Now, Lady Macbeth warns her husband that he is transparent and must learn to '*look like the innocent flower, / But be the serpent under't*'.

She must tread carefully with her husband whom she thinks is '*too full o' the milk of human kindness / To catch the nearest way*'.

In her soliloquy, before his arrival, she talks to her absent husband saying:

> thou wouldst be great;
> Art not without ambition, but without
> The illness should attend it: what thou wouldst highly,
> That wouldst thou holily; wouldst not play false,
> And yet wouldst wrongly win,

but she knows better than to tell these truths to his face. Instead she merely says:

> He that's coming
> Must be provided for; and you shall put
> This night's great business into my dispatch.

By taking the responsibility on herself she trips him into action, hoping to bypass his conscience.

Apart from in his letter to her, the Macbeths never mention the word 'King' when talking of Duncan. Lady Macbeth only uses it once, later in the play, when referring to her husband, and he likewise later and only in the witches' presence; nor do they venture the word 'murder', but skirt round it with euphemisms. She talks of '*This night's great business*' and '*Our great quell*'. Neither can confront the symbolic enormity of killing a king.

Lady Macbeth has been described as more pragmatic, more ruthless and more courageous than Macbeth, but she has summoned these qualities out of necessity, to serve her '*fell purpose*'. Courage breeds courage. She dares heaven itself to prevent her plan, and when no obvious divine intervention is forthcoming she feels omnipotent. However, unlike Macbeth, she does not dare look deep into herself, where she would find a much more fearful creature.

She has also been called unimaginative. I prefer to think that she deliberately narrows her focus, shutting out all speculation about the future in order to act more efficiently in the present. When she begs the spirits to '*unsex me here*' and to '*Make thick my blood; / Stop up th' access and passage to remorse*', she is praying for her natural imaginative susceptibility to be suppressed. For me the journey of the part is the fracturing and final disintegration of that suppression.

In Act I, Scene 5, she needs to see herself as the braver of the pair whose role is to

> pour my spirits in thine ear;
> And chastise with the valour of my tongue
> All that impedes thee from the golden round.

Indeed most of Lady Macbeth's valour lies in her tongue. Words embolden her until they become deeds. As events progress she has less and less to say. Her courage slips as her words dry up.

She does lack imagination in those areas where she lacks the experience of her husband. She has not seen blood shed in battle, nor developed Macbeth's sense of soldierly honour, nor has she his reputation to lose. As a consequence, she thinks she is better equipped for killing than she proves to be. This is neatly illustrated by the contrast between her superficial boldness immediately after the murder of Duncan—

> My hands are of your colour; but I shame
> To wear a heart so white

—and the betrayal of her true reaction in the sleepwalking scene much later:

> Yet who would have thought the old man to have had so
> much blood in him?

When Lady Macbeth welcomes Duncan to the castle she performs the '*innocent flower*' to perfection. This is eased by ritual and courtly language that need give nothing away. The king's gentle compliments are hard to receive, but once that ordeal is passed she can congratulate herself on her smooth success at the first hurdle.

When Macbeth suddenly rushes away from the banquet, Lady M chases him down and goads him with a terrifying desperation. Her power is stuck behind the throne. Only he can do the actual deed. He wants to forget the whole idea but she has her reasons why they cannot possibly drop out now.

A Fruitless Crown

In Act IV, Scene 3, on learning that Macbeth has slaughtered his entire family, Macduff cries out, '*He has no children.*' In Act I, Scene 7, Lady Macbeth says, '*I have given suck.*' Macbeth is tormented by the idea of Banquo being '*father to a line of kings*' while he himself is lumbered with '*a barren sceptre*' and a '*fruitless crown*'. This is all the data Shakespeare gives us on the subject, but from this we constructed a theory that would end up motoring my performance.

According to Holinshed's chronicles, Lady Macbeth had a son by an earlier marriage. To assume that this was the child whom Lady Macbeth had suckled would iron out some contradictions and leave the blame for infertility at Macbeth's door. It would also fuel Lady Macbeth's taunts about her husband's manhood. To begin with it seemed an attractive theory.

One director I spoke to reckoned that Lady M is barren and that '*I have given suck*' is a neurotic fantasy that Macbeth plays along with. In Kurosawa's film *Throne of Blood*, Lady Macbeth is pregnant and loses the child at the banquet.

Every production has to find a playable solution. Scholars may be less concerned. One footnote I read dismissed the question of Lady Macbeth's child or children as 'unprofitable'. That editor did not have to play the part.

Jan Kott is more understanding. On whether or not the Macbeths have children he writes: 'This is not the most important factor in the interpretation of the tragedy, although it may be decisive for the interpretation of their parts by the two principal actors.' We found it to be so as soon as we started to put Act I, Scene 7, on its feet.

Tony had the problem of moving from '*We will proceed no further in this business*' to '*I am settled, and bend up / Each corporal agent to this terrible feat*' in as long as it took us to speak forty-seven lines.

Macbeth's turnaround was my problem too. How was I supposed to persuade him in so short a time? Sarah Siddons decided that Lady Macbeth had to be so 'captivating in feminine loveliness' and have 'such potency as to fascinate a hero... to seduce him to brave all the dangers of the present and... the terrors of a future world'. So sheer sex appeal then? Maybe Siddons could do that, but I didn't feel so sure.

I then voiced my problem about the 'giving suck' line. Was it Macbeth's child? If Macduff is right and Macbeth has no children, then Lady Macbeth is referring to her child by another marriage. Is Macbeth infertile? Is his '*Bring forth male children only*' a realistic suggestion? If they could have more children why is Banquo's fecundity so threatening? These were stumbling blocks, but, as is often the case, the actors' need for a coherent throughline produced answers that were more revealing than if we had not stumbled at all.

In dramatic terms the previous child is a no–no. He plays an important part in the real history so why is he not in the play? Answer: Shakespeare is not interested in him. Forget him then and imagine the infant Lady Macbeth talks of to be Macbeth's and that the child is dead.

This seemed to us the most likely and contained the richest theatrical juice. But how, I protested, could a woman who knows '*How tender 'tis to love the babe that milks me*', and has seen that baby die, even contemplate the thought of dashing an infant's brains out? I had fallen into the trap of seeing this violent image as proof of Lady Macbeth's heartlessness. But once I started to act the scene and feel the desperate energy of it, I understood that the opposite was the case. Lady Macbeth is conjuring the most horrendous sacrifice imaginable to her in order to shame her husband into keeping his pledge. To speak such pain-laden words is in itself impressive, and Macbeth realises what it costs her.

To create the highest stakes possible for the couple in this short but pivotal scene, we decided that the couple had not spoken of the child since its death and that for whatever reasons they could not have any more. I argued for more than one dead child, maybe several—a fairly normal tragedy in Shakespeare's day—which would make her feel truly blighted and perhaps vengeful against the world. In a morning's work we had solved Macbeth's volte-face for Tony, found a deep connection between the two characters, and I had found the heart of Lady Macbeth.

I consulted a bereavement counsellor about the effects on parents of losing a child. In some cases it bonds the couple more strongly than ever, in others the marriage cracks under a mixture of unspoken blame, guilt, and grief not shared in a desire to protect the partner from a double burden. Was I bending things too much to think that Shakespeare does not explain the couple's loss because they themselves cannot speak of it?

At the start of the play might not Lady Macbeth be in a deep depression from which she is rescued by a new-found purpose which might restore meaning to her barren marriage? By fixing things so her husband can be King she can make herself indispensable to him. If she cannot give him an heir at least she can get him the crown.

On Macbeth's return from the war, our director, Greg, discouraged tactile shows of affection (bereavement like theirs can lead to a physical coolness): instead they greeted one another at arm's length. During the pause after '*Never shall sun that morrow see*' a servant brought on a bucket of water, a cloth and a towel, and I set about washing my husband's face and arms. In performance this served several functions: having to shut up in front of the servant increased the tension; it provided a moment of unerotic domestic intimacy; it wiped the blood and grime of battle off Tony's face, thus assisting his quick change into the next scene; and it afforded Lady Macbeth a clearer reading of her husband's face and state of mind. It also set up the theme of hand-washing which is threaded through the play.

Greg helped me tell more of my story in the staging of the next scene, where Lady Macbeth welcomes the king's party. To make up maximum numbers, the whole cast entered and filled the stage, among them Macduff, his young son and Lady Macduff with a baby in her arms. This image of happy families scorches Lady Macbeth for a second. I tried to make this moment register with a well-placed look, which I hoped some of the audience would pick up on and remember.

For rehearsal purposes we gave each scene a title (for example 'Sleepwalking' is easier to identify than 'Act V, Scene 1'). Thus Act I, Scene 7, became 'Cold Feet'. I would listen from the wings as Macbeth in soliloquy reasoned his way out of our pact. It struck me that he was more concerned about his action rebounding against himself and about other people's vilification, than about the morality of regicide or his pity for the King. He more or less states that if there were no consequences to his action he would not hesitate,

> that but this blow
> Might be the be-all and end-all...
> We'd jump the life to come.

So much for the milk of human kindness: he is more worried about covering his back! Or so I thought as I waited to go on. In the wings was the life-like doll that had just been in Lady Macduff's arms. Its weight was disconcertingly real as I held it. It was a useful touchstone for the raw fury that I would have to summon in a few seconds' time.

Macbeth's

> I have no spur
> To prick the sides of my intent, but only
> Vaulting ambition

was my cue in every sense to rush in and spur him on some more. When he breaks it to her that '*We will proceed no further in this business*', she explodes like a primed cannon. She disdains his lame excuse that, having just been honoured, the timing is inappropriate. She confronts him with exactly the faults she had listed behind his back in soliloquy: his wanting something for nothing, his lack of resolve, his cowardice. He hides behind some code of manhood that the audience would not dispute, but she is not having it. She knows his real nature.

In most of us law-abiding citizens the Beast is kept under the control of the Man. To Lady Macbeth this is hypocrisy. 'Act out your fantasies. Own up to the whole of what you are. Anything less is weak,' she seems to say.

Within this interchange lie several important textual clues that are easily missed in the desperate heat of the argument. They provide my sliver of defence against all those who think of Macbeth as a nice guy corrupted by his wife. Examine the evidence. She says (my emphasis):

> What beast was't, then,
> That made *you* break this enterprise to *me?*
> When you durst *do it*, then you were a man...
> Nor time nor place
> Did *then* adhere, and yet *you would make both:*

> They have made themselves, and that their fitness now
> Does unmake you,

and at the end of the speech:

> had I so sworn *as you*
> *Have done to this.*

We have not heard Macbeth swear to anything so it must have happened offstage. There must have been a discussion about doing 'it' at a point before '*time and place*' were fitting; i.e. before Duncan came to stay, ergo before the start of the play, and it was *he* who broke the enterprise to *her*. I rest my case.

Macbeth knows this to be true and is weakening, and at that moment his wife deals her trump card. That is one way of playing '*I have given suck*', or it could be a completely uncalculated outburst that takes even Lady Macbeth by surprise. I chose to play something between the two— something that started as a rational argument but which overwhelmed her in speaking it. Suddenly all her anger and sorrow wells up.

As she sees it, she would have loved to be full of the milk of human kindness, but life has hardened her through no fault of her own. Macbeth's moral equivocation is a luxury that she resents. He can still hold his head up in his field. He receives honours. He may be a brave soldier when the rules are straightforward, but he is a coward in her eyes. He cannot match the courage she has built to face each childless day. As a childless wife she has no status. She feels superfluous and dried up. Nothing less than reigning as his Queen can fill the hole in her life.

Her subconscious throws up the terrible image of killing her child, and Macbeth is won over. Only something this enormous could have got him back on course. His simple '*If we should fail?*' is as good as a promise to Lady M, and having chosen such an emotional interpretation for the previous speech, she (and I) had some recovery problems for the reply, '*We fail.*'

Unbeknownst to me at the time, this line is famously controversial. I would later be grilled about it in after-show discussions. In some editions it is punctuated as a question, in others not. How did I think of it? I answered that I varied the playing of it according to how quickly Lady M bounced back from what she had just gone through. The line contained relief that Macbeth was back on board, a challenge to him not to fail and also perhaps a touch of nihilism: a 'what have we got to lose?' Macbeth might answer 'Quite a lot', but life as it stands has little to offer her.

Then follows her garbled plan. She has barely thought it through. In Act I, Scene 5, she has mentioned 'my *keen knife*'. Now she talks of '*What cannot you and I perform...?*' and of 'our *great quell*' (my emphasis). So who exactly is going to do the killing and how? We shall see how unprepared they are in a few scenes' time. Meanwhile Macbeth, genuinely moved by his wife's force of feeling, rewards her with '*Bring forth male children only.*'

Is he indulging her with hope against hope or is he momentarily blinded by his own?

In the event, it is Macbeth who carries out Duncan's murder in Act II, Scene 2. Lady Macbeth's job is to get the king's bodyguards drunk and ring the bell to alert Macbeth when the time is right. In a rare confidential moment with the audience, Lady Macbeth shows she is not quite the tough nut she would like to be:

> Had he not resembled my father as he slept, I had done't.

Macbeth emerges from the king's chamber, and a hissed '*My husband!*' alerts him to his wife waiting in the shadows. He rushes to join her: '*I have done the deed.*'

They must whisper for fear of waking the house. They are bungling amateurs and trip over one another's words:

MACBETH:
Didst thou not hear a noise?

LADY:
  I heard the owl scream and the crickets cry.
  Did not you speak?

MACBETH:
                    When?

LADY:
                              Now.

MACBETH:
                                        As I descended?

LADY:
                                                        Ay.

MACBETH:
  Hark!

and so on. The panicky rhythms of this passage almost play
themselves.

Then Macbeth starts to crack, his speeches spilling over
with terror. His terror is infectious, but Lady Macbeth
smothers her own panic in an attempt to control his.

  These deeds must not be thought
  After these ways; so, it will make us mad.

He raves wildly on, about a voice crying, '*Macbeth does murder sleep... Macbeth shall sleep no more.*' She stops the torrent
for a moment: '*Who was it that thus cried?*' i.e. 'It's all in your
head. Pull yourself together.'

'*Go get some water,*' she commands, '*And wash this filthy
witness from your hand.*' Then her blood freezes:

  Why did you bring these daggers from the place?
  They must lie there: go carry them; and smear
  The sleepy grooms with blood.

He refuses to look again on the crime. 'Pish!' she thinks. 'I'll
go then. How can you be frightened of the dead and the
sleeping?' She charges back up the stairs (in our production), and Macbeth is left alone with his remorse and his
blood-soaked hands.

In that scene offstage in Duncan's chamber, a scene that but for Macbeth's forgetfulness would not have happened, Lady Macbeth is confronted with the deed she has only talked of. The sight of it loosens something in her mind. From that moment her exterior aplomb will grow more and more brittle until it breaks.

According to a psychiatrist whom Greg consulted, one of the signs of a psychopath is an unflinching reaction when faced with their victim. Had the Macbeths been straightforward 'evil' psychopaths, they would feel no remorse. The fact that Macbeth experiences hallucinations and flashbacks and the fact that Lady Macbeth sleepwalks are signs that they are normally functioning human beings and are therefore more terrifying.

Shakespeare makes the connection between seeing the victim and consequent remorse in several ways. The agents of evil to whom Lady Macbeth appeals dwell in '*sightless substances*' and she begs night to shroud her deeds so '*That my keen knife see not the wound it makes*'. When Macbeth makes his direst resolution to kill Macduff's wife and children he says: '*This deed I'll do before this purpose cool. / But no more sights!*' He knows that accomplishment of the deed requires a moral blindfold. From Duncan's death onwards, Macbeth gets someone else to do the killing while he conducts things by remote control.

After the murder scene, the next time we see the couple they are crowned, and we watch their positions reverse. The dominant Lady becomes the ruler's consort. Macbeth's focus has moved on to Banquo. Duncan's heirs have fled under suspicion of their father's murder, and Banquo is now Macbeth's chief rival. Banquo alone knows the witches' full prophecy, and he also knows Macbeth too well for Macbeth's comfort. Lady Macbeth gets little of her husband's attention. Her one line in Act III, Scene 1, is a mere politeness and seems mainly to serve as an in-joke for Shakespeare.

> If he had been forgotten,
> It had been as a gap in our great feast.

There will indeed be a gap at the feast: Banquo's empty chair.

Macbeth and Banquo warily exchange chat, and Macbeth learns that Banquo and his son will be out riding before dinner. There was a strong suggestion in our production that Banquo was heading off to see the witches. Who is not a little tempted by power once it comes within range, or to let his integrity slip when others are playing a dirty game and seem to be winning?

Lady Macbeth is aware of an atmosphere between the friends. She may even detect a hint of what underlies it. She dutifully takes a step back, allowing her husband to establish his authority. Tony was quite a bit shorter than Joseph O'Connor who played Duncan, so now, wearing the same costume, it did indeed

> Hang loose about him, like a giant's robe
> Upon a dwarfish thief

—a metaphor for Macbeth's kingship spoken by Angus later in the play (Act V, Scene 2).

Macbeth suddenly dismisses the company.

> We will keep ourself
> Till supper-time alone.

'*Ourself*', not '*ourselves*': Lady Macbeth can't help noticing the abrupt cut-off. She hovers, bewildered…

'*While then, God be with you!*' he says, as if telling her 'and that includes you'. As she exits she just catches Macbeth summoning his servant and realises she is being excluded from something important. (It is possible to play Lady M as a knowing accomplice throughout the scene, but this reading soon runs into trouble.)

Before his interview with the men hired to murder Banquo, Macbeth soliloquises on the bitter joke whereby the crown which has cost him his soul in the gaining will be handed on to Banquo's progeny. Listening from offstage I felt an unspoken accusation. If I had been a better mother…

The next scene (Act III, Scene 2, which we dubbed 'Scorpions') was for both of us the most slippery scene in the play. Ostensibly it neither advances the plot nor tells the audience anything they don't already know. The couple use more than usually tender language to one another ('*Gentle my lord*', '*Love… dear wife…*'), but this seemed a smokescreen or a means of control rather than an expression of love. Committing a murder together had bound them in an almost erotic intimacy, but a new lack of trust had crept under their dialogue.

Before they come together in the scene, husband and wife each has a soliloquy which echoes the other's sentiments. In Act III, Scene 1, Macbeth says, '*To be thus is nothing, but to be safely thus*', and separately, in Act III, Scene 2, Lady Macbeth says,

> Nought's had, all's spent
> Where our desire is got without content:
> 'Tis safer to be that which we destroy
> Than by destruction dwell in doubtful joy,

but when, in her presence, Macbeth says,

> better be with the dead,
> Whom we, to gain our peace, have sent to peace,
> Than on the torture of the mind to lie
> In restless ecstasy,

Lady Macbeth does not own up to her own similar fears.

There is already a difference between their states. His soliloquy develops into a plan to ease his anxiety, while hers expresses an emptiness with no remedy. It is a rare confession of despair, which she quickly converts into tough talk for Macbeth's benefit.

> Things without all remedy
> Should be without regard: what's done is done.

Her seeming denial of the problem only alienates him further.

The problem is Banquo, and Macbeth cannot spell it out. But why can't he confide in his wife? Because he has decided on a course and doesn't want her to argue him out of it? Because he no longer trusts her courage and anyway the fewer people involved the better? Because he is about to kill his best friend and cannot look at his own feelings in the mirror of her shocked face? Any of these could be true but Tony needed to answer the question more specifically, and once again a seeming obstacle led us to a deeper layer of truth.

In his letter to his wife in Act I, Scene 5, Macbeth says nothing of the witches' prophecy for Banquo, and there is no other textual indication that Lady Macbeth learns of it later. One reason could be that he wants to shield his wife from the knowledge that their reign is to be a childless dead-end. The fact that the witches have so far got things right makes their prediction for Banquo more likely and the prospect of more children for the Macbeths ever bleaker.

It takes some nerve to hold on to an assumption like this, especially when Shakespeare offers no explicit proof that this is what he had in mind, but it offered us a psychological coherence. The scene which had felt at first like a hiatus ended up propelling us further apart and further into the hell of the play.

As the scene begins both characters want to reconnect, but Lady Macbeth's need is the greater. She is defined by his need for her, and that need has diminished. Because he cannot be totally honest with her, he is starting to go it alone. The balance of power between them has tipped irretrievably. In the reverse pattern to the one which characterised their earlier scenes together, Macbeth has long speeches while Lady M slips in the odd one-liner.

She listens to his outpourings but cannot quite follow their tortuous path. '*We have scotch'd the snake, not kill'd it,*' he says.

Who is the snake? Not Duncan, for they have killed him.

> She'll close and be herself, whilst our poor malice
> Remains in danger of her former tooth.

She gets the general gist that a crime won't lie down, a sense of a harm not yet rooted out, even a sarcastic mockery of her own apparent calm:

> But let the frame of things disjoint, both the worlds suffer,
> Ere we will eat our meal in fear...

She tries to pull him together in her old practical style with '*Be bright and jovial among your guests tonight*', and he seizes on the chance to bring up Banquo's name:

> So shall I, love; and so, I pray, be you:
> Let your remembrance apply to Banquo;
> Present him eminence, both with eye and tongue

(i.e. throwing back her own instruction to him in Act I, Scene 5: '*bear welcome in your eye, / Your hand, your tongue*').

In performance Tony suddenly broke off at this point. Macbeth knows that Banquo won't be at the feast, and he can't go on with the lie to his wife. Tony delivered the remaining

> Unsafe the while, that we
> Must... make our faces vizards to our hearts,
> Disguising what they are

with a sad perusal of my face as if to say, 'And here am I disguising my true self even from *you*!' She clings to her old role of comforter, of rallier, but her grasp is less secure. Her part as co-conspirator seems to have been written out.

Macbeth gives a tiny hint of his plans:

> Thou know'st that Banquo, and his Fleance, lives.

A slight pause while she thinks, 'Have I got this right... ?', and then, more concerned to show her husband that she is as sharp as ever than to know why he would kill his friend, she tentatively offers: '*But in them Nature's copy's not eterne*' (innocent of the irony of the line), which provides Macbeth with the go-ahead he still needs her to give. But when she probes further with '*What's to be done?*', the former '*partner of greatness*' is fobbed off with a patronising

> Be innocent of the knowledge, dearest chuck,
> Till thou applaud the deed.

The Lady Macbeth of earlier scenes would have protested, have wrung an explanation out of him, but now she says nothing for the rest of the scene.

For me this silence fitted the theory that Lady Macbeth's ambition is not ambition for power's sake but for her husband and for their marriage. As far as she is concerned, they have achieved what they wanted but '*Nought's had*', if they cannot enjoy it together. She can put the murder behind her (or she thinks she can), but Macbeth's fretting is destroying everything. If they drift apart, her purpose is lost.

Macbeth seems to soliloquise in front of her, almost unaware of her presence. With a mixture of anger, excitement and dread, she listens and watches from the perimeter while Macbeth stokes himself up for some dreadful deed which she dimly guesses at. Banquo is to die, that much she gathers, but the husband she thought she knew would not kill his closest friend, at least not without her courage to sustain him. Evidently he has moved on.

Not being privy to his motives she is all the more dismayed by the thought of what's to be done. When Macbeth snaps out of his soliloquy he interprets her demeanour as '*Thou marvell'st at my words*', and, as if to prevent her interrupting, continues,

> but hold thee still;
> Things bad begun make strong themselves by ill.

In Tony's performance that '*bad begun*' was loaded with a 'You got me into this. You made me into this murderer', and I/Lady

M felt the sting of his hatred as he swept past me and almost left the stage. At the last minute he turned back to interrupt my perturbed reverie with a brusquely extended hand and '*So, prithee, go with me.*'

Stepp'd in So Far

The jaggedness of this last exit informs the atmosphere at the top of Act III, Scene 4 (or 'Dinner with the Ceauşescus' as we flippantly called it). The lights find the pair sitting stiffly side by side, forearms resting on the table top in four parallel lines. They stare ahead with haunted eyes. In keeping with the rest of the set design this feast was to be Brechtian austere: eight tin bowls awaiting a dribble of soup, some cutlery, a rough loaf with a knife to cut it and six guttering candles providing the only light. Into this gloom crept the somewhat cowed guests, each clutching a wine-filled goblet. Macbeth's is already a nervous court.

Tony's Macbeth jumped to his feet to welcome them and took the chance publicly to offset himself against his wife as the approachable People's King.

> Our hostess keeps her state, but in best time
> We will require her welcome.

'Sorry about my snotty wife,' he seemed to say, mocking her tense attitude though his had been identical seconds before. It was an effective betrayal and a taunt: 'You wanted me to be jolly. You taught me to dissemble. Who's the better at it now?'

But his cockiness is short-lived. Banquo's murderer appears, and the host is forced to leave the table without a toast. When he returns, Lady Macbeth gets her own back, publicly but graciously correcting him, and throwing in the odd guest-pleasing witticism for good measure

> My royal lord,
> You do not give the cheer: the feast is sold

That is not often vouch'd, while 'tis a-making,
'Tis given with welcome: to feed were best at home;
From thence the sauce to meat is ceremony;
Meeting were bare without it.

Macbeth has just had dreadful news: Banquo is dead but his son Fleance has escaped. He nevertheless manages a charming show:

Sweet remembrancer!
Now, good digestion wait on appetite,
And health on both!

But the nightmare will out. With the appearance of Banquo's ghost, Macbeth goes to pieces and his wife briefly returns to her old commanding form. Her rationality (*'This is the very painting of your fear:… / When all's done, / You look but on a stool'*) and her taunts (*'O, these flaws and starts, / Impostors to true fear, would well become / A woman's story'*) quieten Macbeth a little, but with each apparition of the ghost he grows less controllable and lets more and more cat out of the bag.

Despite Lady Macbeth's brilliantly improvised cover-ups the guests are not fooled. Depending on each lord's degree of suspicion, Macbeth is either mad or in deep trouble. How are they to interpret Macbeth's speech into the empty air:

If thou canst nod, speak too.
If charnel-houses and our graves must send
Those that we bury back, our monuments
Shall be the maws of kites.

No one yet knows of Banquo's murder, but Macbeth is already suspected by some of having killed Duncan.

Thanks to Lady Macbeth's efforts Macbeth briefly comes to his senses and apologises to the assembly:

Do not muse at me, my most worthy friends,
I have a strange infirmity, which is nothing
To those that know me. Come, love and health to all.

One night Tony delivered

> which is nothing to those that know me

locking eyes with each guest in turn as if to say, 'Anyone who speaks of this is a dead man.' Thereafter it was the only way to play the line. All pretence was over. An open reign of terror had begun.

Lady Macbeth only knows for certain that Banquo is dead from her husband's overfrequent references to his absence from the feast. She is disturbed by Macbeth's uncalled-for

> Here had we now our country's honour roof'd,
> Were the graced person of our Banquo present

early in the scene, but his later

> I drink… to our dear friend Banquo, whom we miss;
> Would he were here! to all, and him, we thirst

is one bluff too far.

When the ghost finally departs and Macbeth is '*a man again*', Lady M gives him a cold and sarcastic

> You have displaced the mirth, broke the good meeting,
> With most admired disorder.

My Lady Macbeth could not even bring herself to look at her husband, so repelled was she. This provoked Tony brutally to swing me round to face him and punish my hypocrisy.

> You make me strange…
> When now I think you can behold such sights,
> And keep the natural ruby of your cheeks,
> When mine is blanched with fear.

There is no saving the situation now. Lady Macbeth suddenly flips. Like a vicious bitch chasing intruders she barks at the guests to get out. They scuttle away and the couple are left alone together, embarrassed, frightened and furious.

The tone of this last phase of the scene is curiously calm. There is a kind of detached intimacy between husband and wife. There are no recriminations or post-mortems. They have both blown it and there is nothing to discuss. Macbeth can ask the simple question: '*What is the night?*', and she can answer, '*Almost at odds with morning, which is which.*'

They are at a mid-point (indeed the scene comes almost exactly halfway through the play) where night elides with day and their world slips into hell. As Macbeth reasons:

> I am in blood
> Stepp'd in so far that, should I wade no more,
> Returning were as tedious as go o'er.

He is preoccupied with the immediate future. Done Banquo—who's next? Macduff? Why didn't he show up? He half-consults his wife on the matter, but they both know it makes no difference what she answers. Instead she offers her own desultory question: '*Did you send to him, sir?*'

As Macbeth mutters his plans to himself, his wife peruses this stranger for whom she has traded her soul, this serial murderer who could only have taken shape under her guiding hand. His torment leaves her cold. She is drained. Exhausted herself, she suggests '*You lack the season of all natures, sleep.*' In one memorable rehearsal, Tony looked at me and I looked at him and the lameness and absurdity of that line under these circumstances struck us simultaneously, and both of us burst into a terrible giggling. We managed to recreate that moment for every performance.

It was a last flash of togetherness before Macbeth leaves the room to wade deeper into crime and to become better at it:

> Come, we'll to sleep. My strange and self-abuse
> Is the initiate fear that wants hard use:
> We are yet but young in deed.

He doesn't notice that his wife's laughter has shifted into hysteria, a half-crazed whimpering. I did not follow him to bed but took one of the candles from the table to light my separate path. We would not meet on stage again.

Sleep No More

> Sleep shall neither night nor day
> Hang upon his pent-house lid.

Thus the First Witch in Act I, Scene 3, cursing the sailor to punish his wife.

Throughout *Macbeth*, sleep is a yearned-for refuge reserved for the innocent and the dead. On the night of Duncan's murder, Banquo's

> A heavy summons lies like lead upon me,
> And yet I would not sleep

signals a loss of trust. He cannot afford to relax his guard. Duncan innocently gives way to sleep and is murdered in his bed.

To kill a king is one thing, to kill a sleeping king is double sacrilege, and Macbeth is to be punished with sleeplessness. It is the presentiment of this particular form of torture that obsesses Macbeth as he rushes from the scene of the crime.

> Methought I heard a voice cry 'Sleep no more!
> Macbeth does murder sleep', the innocent sleep,
> Sleep that knits up the ravell'd sleeve of care,
> The death of each day's life, sore labour's bath.

Lady Macbeth cannot understand him or she will not. She is more concerned with the real fear of discovery. Her narrow focus is her strength. Later, when her purpose is lost with her love, she will suffer the irony of wakeful sleep. The '*access and passage to remorse*' is unstopped, and like a creature in hell she must live out the actions of her crime till the ultimate sleep relieves her.

Macbeth, whose humanity has been measured by his self-honesty in soliloquy, progressively eschews consideration. At the end of Act IV, Scene 1, he declares: '*To crown my thoughts with acts, be it thought and done*', and with these words he condemns Macduff's family to death. It is as though he has absorbed his wife's lesson and taken it further than she could possibly have intended. Indeed it is the murder of Macduff's wife and children that finally tips Lady Macbeth over the edge.

To soliloquise is to make the audience your friend and through them to have a dialogue with yourself. It keeps a character sane. Lady Macbeth is afforded no such luxury. In the whole play she has four lines of honest reflection on her state (*'Nought's had. All's spent...'*). There are other moments that arguably might be shared with the audience, and Greg offered me these, but to me they felt wrong. Her friendlessness seemed essential. Her sleepwalking is her release. It is her soliloquy, if you like, though sleep itself removes her from self-understanding.

'That William Shakespeare must have done a murder' was the response of a convicted murderer who, in return for helping Tony in his research, had been invited to see *Macbeth* for the first time. He was commenting on the accuracy of Shakespeare's portrait of what we now would call post-traumatic stress disorder. In a modern pamphlet on the subject, I read of a young rape victim who 'could not sleep without a light by his bed'. The doctor who witnesses Lady Macbeth's sleepwalking asks, *'How came she by that light?'* To which the attending gentlewoman answers, *'Why, it stood by her: she has light by her continually*; *'tis her command.'*

Once again I marvel at Shakespeare's psychological modernity. God knows how he did it, but the sleepwalking scene, its placement within the play, its atmosphere, its naturalistic rhythms is one of the most memorable scenes in the canon. It comes after a long spell away from Macbeth's castle. The audience has been transported to the witches' cavern, heard the treble voice of children at Macduff's castle, reeled at their brutal murder, and spent time in England breathing a different air made lighter by the promise of revenge. Now the play is plunged into gloom again.

In a corridor of Macbeth's castle a doctor and gentle-woman lurk in the dark, their faces lit by one candle. The gentlewoman has watched Lady Macbeth for several nights and has heard what she knows she should not. She needs to share her burden with a witness. The scene is charged with danger. Think Stalin's Russia, or some such, where to think a thought can be a death sentence, let alone to speak it aloud.

The doctor and gentlewoman are interrupted in their hushed discussion by the entrance of Lady Macbeth. The actress is given clear stage directions by the whispered dialogue:

—You see, her eyes are open.

—What is it she does now? Look, how she rubs her hands.

—It is an accustomed action with her, to seem thus washing her hands: I have known her continue in this a quarter of an hour.

Then the Lady speaks, and this presents something of an acting dilemma. I wanted the audience to feel they were eavesdropping on Lady Macbeth cocooned in her private hell. Unconscious of listeners, she has no need to project, and if I once started to 'perform' the scene I would lose that reality. On the other hand I had to be heard.

For most of the play Lady Macbeth's has been an acting job. She and the actor playing her must make a few central decisions, block out all other considerations, wind herself up and go. Night after night, like Lady Macbeth herself, I would forget the enormity of her crime and focus on the minute-to-minute crisis of each scene, until the sleepwalking scene knocked down our guard and let the horrors break in.

The jump-cut rhythms of her speech give the effect of an incoherent dream.

Out, damned spot! out, I say!

(*The murder has just taken place and she looks at her hands.*)

One: two: why, then, 'tis time to do't.

(*The murder is yet to be done. She is Macbeth hearing the striking bell.*)

Hell is murky!

(*Her present terror? or his?*)

Fie, my lord, fie! a soldier, and afeard? What need we fear who knows it, when none can call our power to account?

(*Talking down his fear or her own?*)
Then the sudden flashback:

Yet who would have thought the old man to have had so much blood in him,

which gives the doctor his first inkling of what is being talked about. Jump-cut to the next horror:

The thane of Fife had a wife: where is she now?

(*If one thane's wife can be killed, why not another?*)
Then the vividly present vision:

What, will these hands ne'er be clean?

The Macduffs' blood is on her hands too. All Macbeth's crimes are her crimes, even this, for she helped create him. Then another volte-face:

No more o' that, my lord, no more o' that: you mar all with this starting.

It is her own starting that she condemns by transference—another insight into the bravado of her earlier scenes.

The doctor and gentlewoman are terrified at what they are learning. '*You have known what you should not,*' says the doctor of his patient. '*Heaven knows what she has known,*' returns the gentlewoman. They do not guess at what she might have done.

Through the thickness of her sleep Lady Macbeth still smells the blood on her hands and her deepest sighs come with the realisation that '*all the perfumes of Arabia will not sweeten this little hand. Oh, oh, oh!*'

Compare this with Macbeth's speech after Duncan's murder:

> Will all great Neptune's ocean wash this blood
> Clean from my hand? No, this my hand will rather
> The multitudinous seas incarnadine,
> Making the green one red.

The difference being that Macbeth confronts his nightmares while awake.

Despite what they guess at, the doctor and the gentlewoman express their compassion: '*I would not have such a heart in my bosom for the dignity of the whole body.*' The defencelessness of a sleepwalker is pitiable even when she is Lady Macbeth. That is the genius of the scene.

Lady Macbeth's '*Oh, oh, oh!*' is the low point in her nightly repeated cycle. She forces herself out of it with her wonted practicality, commanding her husband (or herself) to

> Wash your hands, put on your nightgown; look not so
> pale.—I tell you yet again, Banquo's buried; he cannot
> come out on's grave.

A further revelation for the onlookers: Banquo too?

> Even so?

Then the nightmare jumps back again in time to Duncan's murder.

> There's knocking at the gate: come, come, come, come,
> give me your hand.

Here I groped for the alarmed doctor's hand. Is she awake or asleep?

Then: '*What's done cannot be undone*'—a modulation on her '*What's done is done*' from the 'Scorpions' scene—and with an infinitely weary '*To bed, to bed, to bed!*', she leaves as

swiftly as she came. The doctor has detected something suicidal in her tone, for he requires the gentlewoman to

> Look after her;
> Remove from her the means of all annoyance,
> And still keep eyes upon her.

But for all their efforts, that bed does indeed become a welcome grave.

Post Mortem

Until I came to play her I did not understand why Lady
Macbeth is supposed to be such a great role. She is out of
the action for huge chunks of the play, has far fewer
speeches than Macbeth and therefore fewer opportunities
to explain herself. Macbeth on his own is unquestionably a
great challenge for an actor, while Lady Macbeth on her own
is less complex. But once you see her as dark twin, mirror,
partner-in-crime to Macbeth, she becomes the great role of
repute.

A year after playing the part I am left with the feeling of
having made a fist-sized dent in a battleship. I had concen-
trated on finding the extremes to which a 'normal' person
can be driven rather than personifying an 'abnormal' psychopath. In the context of our production that was the
coherent path. There are many others.

The 'normal' person approach takes you on a bumpy ride.
I had to dig around for anything I might have in common
with Lady Macbeth, which is not a happy pastime. There is
a fury inside me somewhere, there is a hunger and maybe
even the capacity to kill. Am I unusual? I don't think so. The
point is that the condition of my life does not feed and sustain these qualities. Rage erupts and dies down. Hunger is
kept at bay by a mostly satisfying life, and if I ever want to
kill, the feeling lasts for a second and is quickly quelled by
thinking of the consequences.

So is it only our circumstances that separate me from Lady Macbeth, or does the difference lie in the murkier area of our basic nature? And if as an actress I am able to remould my personality and even to some degree the inner workings of my imagination, how resilient is that basic nature of mine? In order to understand Lady Macbeth's motives I had begun to empathise with her, and empathy blurs moral judgment.

The major difference is that I only *thought* about the things she activated. In that sense perhaps we are all Macbeths, our criminal potential safely dormant until circumstances or a Lady Macbeth whips us up out of our law-abiding complacency.

BEATRICE
A Woman with a Past

As Beatrice with Kirsten Parker (Hero)
Much Ado About Nothing, Royal Shakespeare Company, 2002

This piece was put together recently with the prompt of the transcript of an interview I gave at the time. I go into further detail on Much Ado *in Chapter Seven: 'Two Loves'.*

I played Beatrice opposite Nicholas le Prevost's Benedick in Greg Doran's production of *Much Ado About Nothing* at the RSC in Stratford and later at the Theatre Royal Haymarket in London in 2002 when I was in my early fifties. It was therefore a tale of middle-aged love.

In a context in which unmarried women were viewed as either innocent virgins, whores or old maids, it was refreshing to play a Beatrice who is something in between. If she is a virgin, she is not innocent; and her love/hate for Benedick is a long-standing love/hate exclusively reserved for him, therefore she is no whore. Old maid she may be, but her self-professed scorn for the state of marriage and her one-off originality safeguard her from any pity. In my own life I had had experience of this fragile state and had occasionally worn a similar mask.

Beatrice is a poor relation, we sense, a long-term fixture of Leonato's household, welcome as long as she is useful and amusing.

She may be the leading lady of the play, but in the hierarchy of the family she is the subplot and Hero plays the lead. Hero is the heiress who must be suitably married off and whose honour is prized as highly as her dowry. No one expects Beatrice to marry now, and the fact that she is not on the market frees her to be irreverent, funny and sometimes downright rude.

There is clearly a history between Beatrice and Benedick that has taken place before the play starts. It is never explicit (nor should it be made so if Shakespeare didn't intend it), but the oblique references to it in some of Beatrice's lines were the most delicious to play.

There are so many giveaways as to Beatrice's love for Benedick, and the fact that the audience knows it long before she admits it herself is part of the pleasure of the play.

Benedick provides her with her first motivation to speak in the play. On learning that the soldiers have returned from war and are expected any minute, she asks,

> I pray you, is Signior Mountanto returned from the wars or no?

No one said anything about Benedick. Why bring him up? She gives him a rude name (basically Sir Mountalot) to mask her serious concern as to whether Benedick is alive or dead, and hopes to get away with it.

Only Hero knows who she is talking about:

> My cousin means Signior Benedick of Padua,

and, quickly before anyone can mistake her inquiry for anything romantic, Beatrice races on:

> He set up his bills here in Messina and challenged Cupid at the flight; and my uncle's fool, reading the challenge, subscribed for Cupid, and challenged him at the bird-bolt. I pray you, how many hath he killed and eaten in these wars?

None of these quips is easily conveyed to a twenty-first-century audience, but if your onstage audience seem to find them hilarious, their laughter, the mention of Cupid, and some use of the past tense is enough to indicate that thereby hangs a tale.

So what is the history of Beatrice and Benedick? The actors and director need to cook up a theory even if the audience can never know it. We found a few possible scenarios, but the most helpful one was that at some point in the past, when they were letting their guard down and verging on a loving relationship, there had been a misunderstanding whereby each had interpreted the other as having rejected them. Both pretend to the world and to themselves that they were the dumper not the dumpee. Both are too proud to admit their pain, so they revert to raillery and public scorn.

This 'performance' not only acts as a much-needed shield to protect each of their egos, but it also becomes so publicly entertaining that they feel obliged to please the crowd and keep it up. Like Kate and Petruchio in what I find a less sympathetic play, *The Taming of the Shrew*, they are trapped by the success of their posturing into a habit of mutual dislike. Everyone expects it of them, and they have got to a point where each privately expects it of him- or herself.

Benedick probably never got so far as to consciously think he was in love with Beatrice, while Beatrice, who is a little more in touch with her feelings, deep down recognises the pain in her heart for what it is. It is more fun and more bearable to convert that pain into teasing and that love into dislike.

That is the state of play in their first meeting. This interchange could be played a little aside from the others, but Beatrice's first line to Benedick seems aimed to publicly deflate him while he is on a roll.

> I wonder that you will still be talking, Signior Benedick: nobody marks you.

Benedick is ready:

> What, my dear Lady Disdain! are you yet living?

So is Beatrice:

> Is it possible disdain should die while she hath such meet
> food to feed it as Signior Benedick?

The crowd gathers round them, and they're off!

The speed of their repartee shows they are pitted equally against each other and hang on one another's words. They are certainly not indifferent to one another. The actors tread the line between playful banter and downright nastiness. It is outwardly enjoyable until Benedick cuts it short rather viciously:

> But keep your way, i' God's name; I have done.

Stranded with egg on her face, Beatrice deals him a last blow:

> You always end with a jade's trick: I know you of old.

That line was interesting to play. I could choose from night to night how thinly to disguise her anger and hurt. She could cover very successfully by shouting it after the departing Benedick with an 'I don't care' laugh for those who remained on stage, or she could mutter it to herself for only the theatre audience's ears. Beatrice skates near the edge, teases her audience both on and offstage with hints.

Another example of this comes in Act II, Scene 1, when Don Pedro says,

> Come, lady, come; you have lost the heart of Signior
> Benedick,

and Beatrice replies:

> Indeed, my lord, he lent it me awhile, and I gave him use
> for it, a double heart for a single one. Marry, once before
> he won it of me with false dice, therefore your grace may
> well say I have lost it.

She speaks in prose for most of the play. One always has to find reasons why a character speaks in prose or in verse, and it seems to me that, for Beatrice, prose lends itself to running rings round her meaning, to spontaneity and to dodging the bullet. It felt to me as though she was both wanting to be found out, and absolutely loath to be found out, at the same time. Her jokes are a brilliant mask and also a trap.

It takes the two eavesdropping scenes to reveal Beatrice and Benedick's true feelings to themselves, and it is their private shock (and relief in a way) on discovering their love—and the way in which they 'privately' confess it to the audience—that is so moving and funny. It is also important for all the actors involved in those duping scenes in the garden to remember that each group thinks they are tricking each of the lovers into believing a *lie* that the other is in love with them, and neither group realises till much later that they have in fact revealed the truth.

Benedick blusters as he climbs down from his well-advertised position:

> When I said I would die a bachelor, I did not think I
> should live till I were married.

Beatrice makes her only break into verse to deliver a much humbled and uncharacteristically straightforward soliloquy. It is her only soliloquy in the play, and her only opportunity to tell the audience things she wouldn't dream of revealing to anyone 'inside' the play:

> What fire is in mine ears? Can this be true?
> Stand I condemn'd for pride and scorn so much?
> Contempt, farewell! and maiden pride, adieu!
> No glory lives behind the back of such.
> And, Benedick, love on; I will requite thee,
> Taming my wild heart to thy loving hand:
> If thou dost love, my kindness shall incite thee
> To bind our loves up in a holy band;
> For others say thou dost deserve, and I
> Believe it better than reportingly.

It helped my humiliation that I was soaked from head to foot at the time, hair bedraggled and dress clinging to my every curve. Hero and friends, knowing that Beatrice was eavesdropping on them behind the hedge, thought it would be fun to turn the hose on it and her. (I actually longed for that moment as I was usually pretty warm by that point in the play.)

The Hero/Claudio plot takes over so quickly after Beatrice and Benedick discover their love for one another that Shakespeare denies the latter couple the happy pay-off scene, or at least he postpones it until Act V, Scene 2. Instead, they have to admit their love in the urgent and stressed circumstances of Hero's humiliation at the wedding. Just as Beatrice is beginning to unfurl and put her trust in Benedick, she is reminded of all that she mistrusts about the male species. There is Claudio willing to believe so quickly that his betrothed has been sleeping with another man, and Hero's own father is shockingly quick to believe hearsay above a lifetime's knowledge of his daughter. Both men love their own honour better than they ever love Hero.

Although we know there are plenty of cultures in the world that still uphold these values, a modern Western audience finds the plot quite hard to believe at this point.

By setting the play in Sicily (1940's: Abyssinian campaign, maybe) with visual references that brought to mind the flashbacks in *The Godfather II*, the director Greg Doran placed the play in a world where the dual codes of *omertà* and the Catholic Church set the rules for people's lives. In this context, Claudio's behaviour is believable and Beatrice's bloody-mindedness is justified. It comes from a deep place of fear, however humorously expressed. In such a culture, the bonds between men are stronger than any bond between a man and a woman, and while young women will stick together in mutual protection against this fact, once they marry they are expected to switch their primary loyalty to their man and children.

Beatrice is the outsider, the transgressor against tradition. Paradoxically, it's precisely the resistance to the yoke of marriage that binds Beatrice and Benedick together. It is what makes the relationship distinctive and very modern. They may not want to submit to marriage, but they are getting dangerously old to play the hard-to-get game.

From the moment Beatrice and Benedict admit their love to one another they are free to respect one another's strength of character. In each of them, submitting to love was linked with an idea of loss of power, of control. But having had such a long-drawn-out and often antagonistic courtship, they can be said to really know one another and to have seen the worst of one another. This is very different from the untested and idealistic love between Claudio and Hero, who have really only fallen in love with one another's image and social suitability. Shakespeare deliberately contrasts these two types of relationship, and each plot elucidates the other.

Hero can seem a colourless, rather wimpy character, but in the all-female scenes—the duping scene, Act III, Scene 1, and the scene before her marriage day, Act III, Scene 4—we see the real Hero, uninhibited by the presence of her father or any other man. With her women around her Hero is the alpha female, and the actress gets the chance to show the sparky girl that Beatrice loves, so different from the subdued trophy bride and favourite daughter she is forced to play in public.

By the end of Act IV, Scene 1, the love affair between Beatrice and Benedick has pretty much been resolved, but the play is far from over. The audience has grown to love Beatrice, and Beatrice loves and values Hero. This gives the rest of the play a solemnity, an urgency for lessons to be learnt, justice to be meted out and reconciliation to be earned.

In the midst of this plot unravelling, Shakespeare gives Beatrice and Benedick a lovely scene which doesn't really have any big dramatic purpose other than to delight and satisfy the audience. The couple have still not announced their love to the onstage world, and they have a secluded scene together where they enjoy the relief of dropping the pretence, and basking in one another's love.

It starts with Benedick alone on stage trying to compose a love-poem to Beatrice but giving up because

> I was not born under a rhyming planet.

Beatrice then enters. How are they going to proceed? Immediately we get the mock crossed swords, and Beatrice needs to know whether Benedick has followed through the challenge to Claudio. Benedick answers efficiently:

> Claudio undergoes my challenge; and either I must
> shortly hear from him, or I will subscribe him a coward.

Then he segues straight to the chase:

> And, I pray thee now, tell me for which of my bad parts
> didst thou first fall in love with me?

Then begins a scene that is extremely romantic because of its anti-romanticism. These two know one another of old but are looking at one another in a totally new light.

The banter continues, but there is a world of difference between the veiled nastiness of their earlier exchanges and these playful insults that they both know are expressions of love.

The scene is broken up by Ursula bringing them back to the immediacy of the Hero/Claudio plot, and Beatrice asks,

> Will you go hear this news, signior?

Benedick comes out with the most wonderfully poetic, romantic line:

> I will live in thy heart, die in thy lap, and be buried in thy
> eyes; and moreover I will go with thee to thy uncle's.

Who needs a love poem after that?

Their next meeting is in the final scene. The plot is resolved. Don John has been unearthed as the perpetrator of the whole deception, and Hero has been 'posthumously' proven innocent. Claudio goes through a deep atonement and agrees to marry another woman that has been chosen for him—in itself a bit of a dodgy idea, but Greg worked hard to counter this and to make Claudio's contrition, which can seem way too glib, as sincere as possible.

Everyone is assembled for the occasion when Claudio is to meet his new bride. The women enter all veiled, and Claudio must make his vows to a woman sight unseen. He declares his pledge to the veiled woman; she then lifts her veil; and hey presto she looks the image of Hero! Claudio cries out:

Another Hero!

and Hero neatly responds:

One Hero died defiled, but I do live,
And surely as I live, I am a maid.

Love, tears and reconciliation all round. But there are a few loose ends still to tie up. Benedick imitates the ritual we have just seen and asks the remaining veiled women:

Which is Beatrice?

and Beatrice steps forward.

They have a captive audience for their best act so far. Their power struggles are over. Beatrice no longer feels the need to have the last word, and together they can turn the tables on all the tricks played on them. 'You thought we hated one another; well, surprise, surprise, we love one another.'

It is reminiscent of the final scene in *The Taming of the Shrew* but without that play's problematic ambivalence. This is not a woman's capitulation. This is set to be a marriage of equals who truly know the person they have taken on and don't want them to change.

TWO LOVES
Or, The Eternal Triangle

In which I further touch on the characters of
Ophelia, Portia, Beatrice, Helena, Viola,
Imogen and Cleopatra

As Viola with Donald Sumpter (Orsino)
Twelfth Night, Royal Shakespeare Company, 1987

In 2011 I was commissioned to contribute a piece on any aspect of Shakespeare I wanted to explore, for a book called Living with Shakespeare: Actors, Directors, and Writers on Shakespeare in Our Time. *It was edited by Susannah Carson for the American publishers, Vintage. I have edited it for the purposes of this book.*

Two loves I have of comfort and despair,
Which like two spirits do suggest me still:
The better angel is a man right fair,
The worser spirit a woman colour'd ill.

Sonnet 144

It has been, and probably ever will be, up for debate as to whether Shakespeare's Sonnets are autobiographical, but Sonnet 144 gave rise to a line of thought in my own mind whilst playing many of Shakespeare's heroines. In all but a few cases, I found myself as a character in competition with another man for the love of the hero. I decided to try and chart the variations in this triangular tension through the plays I had performed in and perhaps even get closer to Shakespeare's own feelings.

Romeo and Juliet was the earliest of Shakespeare's plays that I played in, by which I mean the earliest written

(1593–5) rather than the first one I performed. I played the part for BBC Radio when I was thirty but could *sound* a convincing thirteen. However young, Juliet seems more mature throughout the play than Romeo, who is to a certain extent dragged back by the boy culture which he is part of. Mercutio and his band of friends mock him for his lovesick moping over a woman, first Rosaline, and later Juliet (Act II, Scene 4).

> Alas poor Romeo! he is already dead; stabbed with a white wench's black eye; shot through the ear with a love-song; the very pin of his heart cleft with the blind bow-boy's butt-shaft.

Romeo is seen as deserting the gang, and this theme is developed further in the later play *Much Ado About Nothing*, when Benedick's soldier companions ridicule his succumbing to love and marriage with Beatrice. In both these examples there is a tinge of jealousy and a fear of losing their mate to another mysterious world that they do not understand and therefore need to despise—the world of women and marriage, which they feel necessarily leads to a betrayal of the buddy culture in which they are stuck.

Much Ado was written in 1598, at about the same time that Sonnet 144 is thought to have first been circulated amongst Shakespeare's closest friends. When I played Beatrice at the RSC in 2002, I felt very aware of the tussle that Benedick was going through between the strong male bonding to his army mates, and his tentative gropings towards a complicated grown-up heterosexual love for Beatrice. Shakespeare deliciously plays with Benedick's pride in his soliloquy in Act II, Scene 3, when he has just overheard that Beatrice is in love with him and has to wriggle out of his own past pledge to remain a bachelor (Act II, Scene 3):

> I have railed so long against marriage: but doth not the appetite alter? A man loves the meat in his youth that he cannot endure in his age.

Even at this point he does not quite admit that he could possibly love Beatrice but couches his change of heart from male love to female in the more or less honourable excuse: '*The world must be peopled.*' Maybe this was the philosophy of Shakespeare's day. Physical love could be homo- or heterosexual, but the latter had to be surrendered to in the end in order to keep the species going. Marriage was a biological duty or imperative, while one's true tastes and heart might lie elsewhere.

With this thought in mind, I found a way through the almost impossible 'Kill Claudio' moment in Act 4, Scene 1. At the prompting of the malevolent Don John, Claudio has slandered Hero and left her at the altar. Beatrice is distraught for her friend's sake, and when Benedick entreats, '*Come, bid me do any thing for thee,*' she responds with the unexpectedly harsh, '*Kill Claudio.*' For me, rather than it being simply an irrational incitement to murder, the line became a different kind of test, whose subtext was: 'Prove to me that you are willing to cut out from your heart the strutting misogynist ethos of Claudio and your old gang.' At the same time I had to confront the fact that Beatrice is no pacifist saint. She herself would show no mercy to Claudio: '*O God, that I were a man! I would eat his heart in the market-place*', or at least this is her boast, whose main purpose is to throw down a gauntlet to Benedick challenging him to be a 'proper' man, to be as brave and avenging as she would be if she could.

Benedick passes his test with flying colours and without having to actually kill Claudio. All the worlds are reconciled and the villain Don John is punished in the end. Only the ambiguous figure of Don Pedro, whose love for both Benedick and Beatrice is never quite expressed, remains unresolved. Benedick thinks he has the solution: '*Prince, thou art sad; get thee a wife, get thee a wife.*' Somehow we feel that won't fix Don Pedro's 'problem'.

'Sad' is the word that strikes one when considering Antonio in *The Merchant of Venice* (1596). It is sometimes thought that Shakespeare played this eponymous role in a play where the other characters, especially Shylock, eventually eclipse the person who had started as the central figure. In fact, Antonio opens the play with '*In sooth, I know not why I am so sad.*' Here again is a triangular relationship between an older man, a younger man and a woman.

Antonio and the heiress Portia are both in love with Bassanio. Bassanio himself is caught between his loyalty to a man who has mentored and cherished him and whom he knows fairly intimately, and a woman whom he finds beautiful and amazing (and yes, is extremely rich), who has the mystique of a distant shimmering object that he knows very little about.

The adventurer in him is what both his lovers like about him. Bassanio dares to have a go at Portia's dead father's test—a suitor is presented with three caskets; if he chooses the right one he wins Portia's hand, and if he does not he must remain celibate for the rest of his life—and he chooses the right casket. Just as he and Portia are about to celebrate his success, he hears of Antonio's plight—the merchant has lost his ships and is being held to ransom by Shylock to pay him what he owes. Without a moment's hesitation, Bassanio rushes to Antonio's side. Portia, hurt by this but nothing daunted, decides to disguise herself as a lawyer and defeat Shylock in court. The realisation is painful to her that it is only by saving Antonio that she will find the way to Bassanio's heart.

After her success in the courtroom, there is a key scene between the disguised Portia and Bassanio where she tries to get him to give her the ring that he promised Portia never to remove. He manages to hold out and refuse to surrender it, and then Portia leaves, presumably well pleased that her betrothed has kept his pledge.

Seconds later Gratiano, Bassanio's friend, runs after her with the ring. Bassanio has changed his mind. All Antonio had had to say was '*My Lord Bassanio, let him have the ring: / Let his deservings and my love withal / Be valued against your wife's commandment*'. Portia has no words here to express it, but we must assume her hurt on realising how little it had taken to swing Bassanio's loyalty away from his wife and back to the other man in the triangle.

In the fifth act of *The Merchant* the intricate knot of complex loyalties is exposed and no one escapes without a sting. Bassanio has to face his own confusion of emotions vis-à-vis his admiration for a young boy lawyer who showed exceptional skill, initiative, courage and intelligence, and to whom he is indebted for the life of his friend, and he must digest the fact that this boy was one and the same as his supposed golden wife in her gilded Belmont cage. Portia has to live with her husband's uncertain sexuality, and Antonio has to stand by and witness and eventually bless the heterosexual bond between his beloved Bassanio and the woman who saved his life.

With *Hamlet* and *Troilus and Cressida* (both written in or around 1601) Shakespeare enters a darker, more misogynist phase. Imagine playing Cressida, reviled for her betrayal of Troilus, with no self-justifying speech to explain her actions to the audience or to posterity. It is as if Shakespeare abandons his own feisty creation like an unforgiving parent who has changed his mind about her worth.

Imagine, too, playing Ophelia, and being told that

> The power of beauty will sooner transform honesty from what it is to a bawd than the force of honesty can translate beauty into his likeness,

or

> If thou dost marry, I'll give thee this plague for thy dowry: be thou as chaste as ice, as pure as snow, thou shalt not escape calumny. Get thee to a nunnery, go: farewell.

Remember that you are in love with the speaker (Hamlet), who has become, in most cultures of the world, the most eloquent voice of humanity's psychological condition, and imagine being given practically nothing to say in your defence. Knowing, moreover, that 'the noble' Hamlet's treatment of Gertrude is similar, you can see how one starts to wonder whose side Shakespeare is on.

In fact I have turned down the part of Gertrude more than once because she seems to me to be even more muzzled than Ophelia, who at least breaks out into a form of self-expression in her madness. Gertrude is told by her son that she is too old for sex:

> You cannot call it love for at your age
> The hey-day in the blood is tame, it's humble
> And waits upon the judgment.

With these words the child seeks to control the mother. This is a love triangle with an Oedipal slant. Hamlet wishes to kill his rival Claudius for usurping his dead father's place not only on the throne but also in his mother's bed. Not able to deal with his own complex emotions, he is vicious and oppressive towards both the women he loves, and in the most famous play in the world the woman's voice is barely heard.

So it is that sometimes, while 'inhabiting' a Shakespearean heroine, we feel to be on the receiving end of a comment about our own sex that is distancing and alienating. Almost worse are the times when these comments are forced out of our own mouths. We are required to say, for example, as Viola:

> How easy is it for the proper-false
> In women's waxen hearts to set her forms!
> Alas, our frailty is the cause, not we!
> For such as we are made of, such we be,

or as Cressida:

> Ah, poor our sex! This fault in us I find,
> The error of our eye directs our mind,

and even Cleopatra chides herself for being

> No more but e'en a woman.

With these self-condemnatory words, we and our characters are made to endorse a negative male attitude which is never quite disowned by Shakespeare himself.

Maybe I should give him a break here. In *As You Like It* (1599) the older male cynic, Jacques, is marginalised at the end and Shakespeare seems genuinely to love Rosalind. Likewise in *Twelfth Night* (1601) he spreads his gentle ridiculing of the madness of love even-handedly between both sexes and gives Viola the voice of insight among the self-deluded. She is the fresh breath of air in a pit of insanity. She has the audience's ear and they are always on her side. One feels Shakespeare's approval carrying her along.

In *Twelfth Night*, Shakespeare reaches a kind of apotheosis in his expression of sexual ambiguity. It is not so much a case of a love triangle as of several overlapping and contiguous love triangles. Viola is in love with Orsino and, disguised as his page Cesario, she must woo her own rival, Olivia; Olivia falls for the 'boy' Cesario and meanwhile Orsino, who is supposed to be in love with Olivia, must face his ambisexual attraction to his page. The play is often blissfully funny. It is painful and perfect.

I wasn't thinking along those lines at the time, but the paradox is that as the disguised Viola I was acting out the young man in the triangular tussle between an older man (Orsino), a young man (Cesario), and a woman (Olivia). I even spoke lines that echo the recurrent theme of the Sonnets when Viola/Cesario chastises Olivia with

> Lady, you are the cruellest she alive
> If you will lead these graces to the grave
> And leave the world no copy.

The beauty of it is that Viola uses her insight into the female condition to get close to Olivia, and it is that which draws Olivia to fall in love with her. Viola is the catalyst by which Orsino shifts from his unrequited objectifying and idolisation of Olivia to a more open-eyed mature love for Viola. That this transition has to be worked through the agency of a boy catalyst is a bittersweet solution. Having acted out a kind of man-to-man intimacy, Viola has had a privileged glimpse into the male world and knows Orsino thoroughly. Orsino looks at women with a fresh eye on learning that the boy he favoured and confided in was actually a woman. A real woman. By becoming her own rival in the guise of a young man, the woman achieves her love, and despite an unresolved twinge of pain, with Viola knowing Orsino almost too well, this marriage looks to be set fairer than most.

Helena in *All's Well That Ends Well* (written around 1604) is caught up in a rivalry with Parolles for the love of Bertram. It is hard to know where Shakespeare stands on any of these characters. He makes Helena a bit of an odd-ball, and shows little sympathy for either of the men in the love triangle. Bertram is an arrogant, privileged young pup, while Parolles, his best friend and accomplice in deserting Helena, while enjoying the audience's affection and laughter for much of the play, is finally shown up as a shallow swindler. With all the more revered and upright characters—the Countess, the King, Lafeu the old courtier, and even the Fool, not to mention all the characters she meets in Italy—endorsing Helena's cause and expressing approval of her character, it would seem that Shakespeare himself was on her side.

To inhabit a character created by Shakespeare is a curious experience. To begin with, there is the inescapable fact that he never intended a woman to play the role, and, as I mentioned earlier, there is sometimes a feeling of discomfort at inhabiting the object of misogyny where presumably a boy player would have felt none.

There is one scene in *All's Well*, for example, in which Parolles speaks to Helena with a disinhibited crudeness quite unlike any other I can think of outside the brothels of *Measure for Measure* or the Boar's Head in Cheapside. Perhaps because Helena is not well-born herself, Parolles feels he can speak to her with an indelicacy he would not have used with a noblewoman. He tells her, for instance, that

> Virginity breeds mites, much like a cheese; consumes itself to the very paring, and so dies with feeding his own stomach... Keep it not: you cannot choose but lose by it.

He continues:

> Virginity is like one of our French withered pears, it looks ill, it eats drily; marry 'tis a withered pear. Will you anything with it?

Helena is not devoid of quips and parries to Parolles's digs against her virginity, but to sit and listen to such lines one feels with the character: mocked, insulted and dirty. On the other hand, one can also feel in a strange way to be more equal, let in on the secrets of a club, albeit a pretty horrible one. From one of his closest associates, Helena is being educated as to the male ethos which Bertram is a part of, and it is all useful stuff to a relatively sheltered girl.

Eventually Parolles is exposed as a coward in a scene which completely opens Bertram's eyes as to the true nature of the man he has been emulating, and from this point onwards, uncoupled from his blokeish partnership, Bertram is set free on the long (and still tricky) path to redemption and into the arms of his loving wife.

Imogen in *Cymbeline* (1610) falls victim to Iachimo's desire to drive a wedge between a man and a wife, for who knows what personal reasons of his own. The name Iachimo shares its etymological root with that of Iago in *Othello*

(1603/4), a fellow destroyer of marriage whose motives we never learn.

Neither man is indifferent to the goodness and beauty of the woman they are intent on destroying. Indeed they seem to be partly in love with them. Unlike Desdemona, Imogen survives to live with and digest the misogyny which the plot exposes in her husband's heart. Like her, we are left with the question: How could Posthumus so easily believe the worst of his wife and decide to have her killed without ever giving her the chance to defend herself? And what motivates Iachimo? He has nothing personal against Imogen, never having met her when he forges his plan, and he barely knows Posthumus. One asks the same questions in the Othello/Iago/Desdemona triangle and to some extent in the Polixenes/Leontes/Hermione triangle in *The Winter's Tale* (1611).

The answers must lie somewhere in the mutual ignorance of men and women as to the nature of the other. The physical attraction or biological compulsion towards someone one barely understands, leaves great opportunity for suspicion, and for the projection of one's own self-hatred on to the 'other'. The man can too easily blame the woman for his uncomfortable feeling of powerlessness.

Mutual mistrust is central to the relationship of Antony and Cleopatra, and one could say that Enobarbus makes up a third in the triangle. He is the mediator who loves Antony and is possibly in love with Cleopatra, but is in competition with her for Antony's soul. In many ways they are mirror images of one another. Both love the powerful Antony, both witness his deterioration with sadness, one deserts him and one has a mind to.

Enobarbus is a shrewd social observer and the chronicler of his age, a satirist who often expresses the misogyny of the times and of an army man. '*Between them* [women] *and a great cause, they should be esteemed "nothing".*' But he is also a wise and broadminded man who finds Cleopatra infuriating but captivating and understands her in a way that Antony doesn't quite.

Enobarbus is one of my favourite characters and perhaps—as Cleopatra, as an actor, and even as a woman—I find that I want his approval.

I want Shakespeare's approval, too. Shakespeare is supposed to be invisible and undetectable within the lines of his plays, but just occasionally when you speak his lines in character, you feel you almost know the man and inevitably want to know him better.

I am trying to resist the too definitive idea that the 'real' Shakespeare is to be found in the Sonnets. We must allow him his shifts in attitude, his ambivalence, the changes of heart that we all experience as we grow older ('*A man loves the meat in his youth that he cannot endure in his age*'), and so I have to lay aside my aching curiosity and accept that I can never know the man whose words I (mostly) love to speak and hear.

CLEOPATRA
The Consummate Actress

As Cleopatra
Antony and Cleopatra
Royal Shakespeare Company, 2006

I wrote this chapter recently with the benefit of ten years' hind-sight. It was a welcome opportunity to revisit this extraordinary woman.

The Daunting Task

Cleopatra is the pinnacle of the female actor's Shake-spearean repertoire. We do not have the male actor's lifespan from Romeo to Hamlet, Macbeth, Timon and King Lear. Cleopatra is the end of our road, and she died aged 39.

I had had a break from the RSC through the 1990s and had been acting in modern plays, on television and in films, but by 1999, with the offer of playing Lady Macbeth, my appetite for Shakespeare had returned. After the intensity of Lady Macbeth I relished the lightness of Beatrice, which I went on to play a few years later, and both these parts expressed some part of myself. But where to go next? There was only Cleopatra left to truly challenge and advance me further, but I didn't feel drawn to her, and I didn't feel any connection with her. So I had never put myself forward to try her, and had even turned down the role not long before I finally accepted Greg Doran's offer to play her at the RSC in 2006.

What changed me? It was mainly the trust I had built up with Greg. He is the most unfussy director, who builds everything from the text and imposes no tricks or conceits that are not supported by the clues and givens in Shakespeare's language. So I put my first toe in the Nile, so to speak, by saying yes to Greg. But then there was the problem of who would play Antony.

There are some parts that male actors shy away from because they have a reputation for being unrewarding or dull. Given the choice (and male actors do have the choice) they would rather not play what they perceive as a supporting role to a more eye-catching female role. One actor I asked to play Judge Brack to my Hedda Gabler turned it down because 'It's her play'. At least he was honest. (If women had that luxury, we might turn down Lady Macbeth, Gertrude or Goneril because 'It's *his* play'.) Luckily some actors have more sense, and I have been blessed with some great acting partners: one of the greatest was Patrick Stewart, who positively wanted to play Antony.

Patrick had played Enobarbus a couple of times, a part that is sometimes thought to be the best male role in the play. By playing the character who best understands Antony, he had gained insights into the part, and now, after years of Hollywood stardom, he saw a chance to get back to Shakespeare and play a role he had developed an ambition to perform. Luckily for me.

How do you approach playing a woman who reputedly stops the heart and eclipses the reason of every man she meets? Who has Julius Caesar eating out of the palm of her hand? To me Cleopatra was Elizabeth Taylor, Ava Gardner, Mata Hari, the erotic, black-eyed woman on Edwardian postcards, impossible for me to get near. However, once I did my research, I found that nowhere in the play or in any historical account is Cleopatra described as beautiful. In fact any existing images of her make her look rather heavy-browed and long-nosed. Hooray! Yes, but on second thoughts *not* hooray because that meant she managed to pull the men *despite* not being beautiful. That means she possessed some indefinable sexual ingredient, the X-factor which you either have or have not got and which is something beyond the art of acting.

What I did have were Shakespeare's words, and they became my largest sexual attribute. They say the brain is the largest sex organ in the body, and her words were of infinite variety. Playful, grandiose, self-dramatising, switchback, heart-breaking, infuriating and unpredictable. I knew that my best chance of convincing an audience that men might fall at my Cleopatra's feet would be to get behind those words, the switches of mood, the reach of her imagery, the energy and the emotion to be inferred from her rhythms. And if I could bring all that off the page and on to the stage, I wouldn't need to fulfil every man's fantasy with my physique or some 'X' ingredient. Getting behind those words would be a tough enough task, but at least it was one that could be worked at, whereas one's physical attributes are more immutable.

What I also had was the real experience of a woman on the cusp of old age, with all the contradictions that presents. On the one hand still in touch with a youthful energy and physicality, and on the other the consciousness that, as I joked at the time, 'this may be the last time I play the love interest'. Both Patrick and I are fairly fit and athletic—which I am rarely required to demonstrate—so we both used that quality of physical energy and enjoyment wherever we could, and indeed I haven't had and don't expect to have another chance to run around the stage barefoot or ever again to leap into a stage lover's arms.

In Love with Love

> I shall see
> Some squeaking Cleopatra boy my greatness
> I' the posture of a whore.

Cleopatra knows that plays will be written about her, and she wants to be in control of the record of her life. It is often the case with Shakespeare's heroes and heroines that they are self-consciously acting out their own story. Nowhere is this more the case than in *Antony and Cleopatra*. Both protagonists are in love with their own love story, and they play it out very publicly in front of three layers of audience: the audience of the court and servants on stage with them, the audience who have paid to see the play, and the audience of the gods to whom they feel intimately related and who lend them the importance and consequence that they believe they deserve.

When we did *Macbeth*, Greg Doran had consulted a psychiatrist about the definition of a psychopath and whether he thought the Macbeths could be described as such. He also helped us identify the *folie à deux* syndrome that linked the couple in their crime. This same psychiatrist helped Greg with *Antony and Cleopatra* and corroborated Patrick's theory that much of Antony's erratic behaviour and loss of judgment could be explained if he were an alcoholic. Cleopatra also fulfils the pattern of a codependant and enabler, as she encourages his maddest schemes, mainly, one senses, in order to prop up the collapsing hero and their collapsing relationship.

Greg then asked the psychiatrist what psychological profile might fit Cleopatra? The answer came back that she was an almost textbook narcissist.

I leapt to my computer and looked up examples of narcissists and found them to be people who, far from being in love with themselves, feel invalid unless other people praise them. Such people are in need of a perpetual audience—

even if that audience is themselves in a mirror—and are given to disproportionate notions of their own importance, swinging from the depths of insecurity to ridiculous self-aggrandisement. It is as though they cannot bear to be alone and face the silence that might echo their own inconsequentiality. I also read that at the more insane end of the spectrum they have delusions of grandeur, imagining themselves to be Napoleon or Jesus, Joan of Arc or Cleopatra. 'But she *is* Cleopatra!' I shriek. Very confusing for her, just as it might be confusing to be a Michael Jackson or a Madonna. What do *they* think when they are alone and look in a mirror?

I had noted over the years that a large part of the X-factor, star quality, or whatever you want to call it, is the desperate *need* to be a star. Whatever its psychological source, that need to have power over people can be developed into a self-fulfilling art, the art of playing with people's desire. This provided a helpful insight into the desperation that lies at the heart of the play. A desperation for both lead characters to hang on to one another, and to the political and sexual power their combined personalities have achieved and which is on the wane from the beginning of the play.

The actual Antony and Cleopatra *were* undoubtedly important on the world stage, and their love affair *did* have bearing on the future course of history. At the point where Shakespeare takes up their story, Antony's reputation as a major player and his stake as co-ruler of the Roman Empire were extremely fragile. He was perceived by Rome as someone who had gone native in Egypt and had surrendered his reason to the exotic and erotic otherness of that country as embodied by Cleopatra. As for Cleopatra, her Empire depended for its very existence on Rome's need for her abundant harvests and geographical position. If she proved too much trouble in making a 'strumpet's fool' of their great Mark Antony, she could easily be got rid of, the 3,000-year-old Egyptian Empire would wither and be subsumed into the Roman one. Cleopatra personally identifies with her country, naming herself the goddess Isis, and Antony on his deathbed personifies her as the country itself ('*I am dying, Egypt*'), and it is as near to the truth as of any character that her fate and the fate of her country are one and the same thing.

This narcissism that is partly founded in truth became for me a helpful track through the play. From the opening scene she is showing off to the court that she still has it in her. Antony is long expected back in Rome, but she has the power to keep him by her side. Her temperamental storms are done for show, to tantalise Antony and to amuse her court. She even advises one of her women that the best way to keep a man is to be contrary. She gives the order to send a message to Antony and '*If you find him sad, / Say I am dancing; if in mirth, report / That I am sudden sick: quick and return.*'

When her woman, Charmian, challenges Cleopatra's methods and suggests that the better tactic would be to '*In each thing give him way, cross him in nothing*', Cleopatra retorts: '*Thou teachest like a fool; the way to lose him*', giving Charmian the benefit of her years of experience of keeping the balance of power by playing one mighty leader off against another.

It has to be added here that Shakespeare was certainly describing another narcissistic ruler nearer to home in his own late Queen Elizabeth. Like Cleopatra, Elizabeth used her sexual armoury to rule a small nation surrounded by potential enemies. Elizabeth did this by playing a nail-biting game of time-delays and promises of marriage to foreign princes that she never meant to fulfil. Like Cleopatra, Elizabeth was a marvellous theatrical self-propagandist, throwing banquets and putting on masques and pageants that would leave Cecil B. DeMille floundering. Like Cleopatra, Elizabeth appropriated the imagery of a popular goddess, or the equivalent, by styling herself as the Virgin Queen/the Virgin Mary, thus unifying all the disparate factions in the country and sealing her authority by tying it in to God's. Also, like Cleopatra, Elizabeth grew up in danger of her life, her very existence being a potential threat to other factions that included close family members. Both had murderous fathers whose memories they worshipped.

When I played Cleopatra I had only just finished playing Elizabeth in Schiller's *Mary Stuart*, and I was steeped in her history. Although I recognised the crossovers between the two women, I was determined to emphasise the differences in their personalities, because I always want to play a contrast to whatever I have just played. Schiller's Elizabeth is buttoned-up and self-controlled, a shrewd politician, almost one of the men. Shakespeare's Cleopatra is outlandish, passionate and impulsive. Shakespeare downplays the intellect and political acumen that the real woman possessed, in favour of perpetuating the myth of the gypsy-whore whose power over men was so irresistible that even the great Mark Antony succumbed.

Once you start to look, Elizabeth is everywhere in Shakespeare's plays, albeit judiciously well-disguised. In *Macbeth*, as Greg Doran pointed out, the Macbeths as a composite are a portrait of the barren Elizabeth whom power corrupts and who successfully gets rid of her closest rival to the throne, Mary Stuart, just as Macbeth gets rid of Banquo. In both cases the bitter irony is that it is the descendants of that rival (the Stuarts/Banquo's progeny) who next inherit the throne and start a new and lasting dynasty. Similarly, when I played Henry IV (see Chapter Ten) I had a memory of Elizabeth haunted by the guilt of having killed a rival and a fellow royal in order to maintain a grip on the throne, however insecure.

By the way, I think I can boast that I am one of the few actors, if not the only one, who has played both the King and the Queen of England.

A Flawed Woman

Cleopatra's playfulness in the opening scenes of the play, as well as her stagey tantrums, mask a genuine insecurity. In the first scene between Antony and Cleopatra the audience is immediately introduced to a pattern in their relationship. An outside agent enters: a messenger from Rome with a summons for Antony to come back to Caesar's side. In front of their audience of attendants, Antony feigns a lack of interest, refuses to hear the news from Caesar and goes back to canoodling with Cleopatra. Their love is boundless and mega-important. Rome can sink into the Tiber for all Antony professes to care. Cleopatra seems to smell a rat. She has sharp instincts, and her mind races to her biggest fear: that the double draw of Caesar and of Antony's wife Fulvia will outweigh Cleopatra's own attractions and pull Antony back to Rome; that she will lose him, and thereby her link to power, forever. The best way to get Antony to stay with her is to order him to read the message while at the same time taunting him with his kowtowing, his thraldom to both his wife's tongue and to the boy Caesar. This in turn makes Antony rebel even more strongly, and he grabs at the idea that he and Cleopatra should disguise themselves and go and people-watch in the streets—an escapist, childish pastime he knows will distract them and bring them close together. They are both grasping at straws, trying to put off the inevitable. They are like middle-aged teenagers.

When Antony does eventually go back to Rome when his wife Fulvia dies, Cleopatra is left with her smaller audience: her coterie of female servants and eunuchs. With them she can be more candid. Cleopatra's team buoy her up, keeping the sexual relationship alive and present, fantasising about where Antony is and what he is doing, imagining him riding his horse: '*Oh happy horse to bear the weight of Antony.*' Hilarity all round. It is like being backstage with the leading actress and her dressers and understudy.

But in that intimate setting comes a bit of honest truth. In our production I suddenly ripped off the black-haired wig with the emblematic 'Cleopatra' cut that I had been wearing from my first appearance and revealed my own hair beneath, which had been treated to look thin and scrappy. Cleopatra looks in the mirror and invites her coterie/audience to imagine this woman they see before them—who is '*with Phoebus' amorous pinches black and wrinkled deep in time*'—as having once been '*a morsel for a monarch*', and one who would cause great Pompey to '*die with looking on his love*'. She is like an ageing film star, but without the scrapbook or movie archive to prove she was once something great.

Although I have never set many of my eggs in the 'sexual allure' basket, I can still relate to some of Cleopatra's fear of getting old. I played Cleopatra in my fifties. Cleopatra died at the age of thirty-nine and to her that was probably the equivalent of fifty to me. Actually, disbelief rather than fear is the predominant sensation when confronting one's ageing face in the mirror. Can this old woman possibly be *me*? And I am again reminded of Elizabeth I, who was described by Sir Walter Ralegh as 'A lady surprised by time'. Elizabeth and Cleopatra may be empresses and queens but they are also mortal women, and I can bring that more mundane aspect on to the stage with me and give them flesh and form.

Elizabeth is purported to have written the poem, 'When I was fair and young', the musings of an old lady looking back and regretting the number of times she rebuffed suitors when she was beautiful and now is left alone. Who knows who might have read that poem? If Shakespeare did, he knew how Cleopatra might look back on her '*salad days*' when she was '*green in judgment, cold in blood*'. It is the midlife cry of men and women alike. Shakespeare would have understood it in his early forties, and in his portrait of both Antony and Cleopatra he shows his sympathy with their fleeting power.

Cleopatra keeps a grip on her household through contrariness and unpredictability. It is a petty form of power, but entertaining to play and to watch. Just when Charmian thinks she has permission to chime in with Cleopatra about how wonderful Julius Caesar was, she is slapped down by Cleopatra's '*Be choked with such another emphasis! / Say, the brave Antony.*' Charmian is her senior handmaiden and as such occasionally tests the limits of how much truth can be hinted at. She is smartly silenced by Cleopatra, but not before the audience has had a glimpse of her mistress's weakness.

Greg Doran is a naturally democratic director who, wherever possible, irons out the hierarchy built in to so many of Shakespeare's plays. I may have been the alpha lioness on stage, but everywhere else I was equal with the rest of the cast, and our mutual trust and enjoyment of one another helped greatly in creating a believable household. You can *play* the cruel and despotic diva without having to *be* one, and you will have a lot more fun on stage.

I was aware that what I call the 'Don't Shoot the Messenger' scene, when a hapless servant brings Cleopatra the news that Antony has married Octavia, is written as a comic scene, but at the same time I found it hard to get past the fact that Cleopatra is genuinely shattered by the news. As a politician she would have totally understood the expediency of Antony marrying Octavius's sister, but as a woman this is a terrible threat. Antony will now have a family thousands of miles away across the sea. Rome has won him back, and her hold over him is weaker than ever. After the comedy of the scene, Shakespeare has Cleopatra genuinely collapse with grief, but he also knows the audience will laugh because he has let them know what Cleopatra doesn't yet know. The audience has just heard Antony say '*I will to Egypt: / And though I make this marriage for my peace, / I' the east my pleasure lies.*' It's all going to be okay. I had to un-know that and reach for genuine desperation and allow the audience to laugh at my histrionics.

The next time we see Cleopatra, when the servant comes back for further cross-examination about Octavia, I could have genuine comic fun with Shakespeare's rhythms and send up Cleopatra's vanity. Every piece of information Cleopatra learns about Octavia she manages to spin into a negative, so a woman who is not particularly tall and speaks with a low voice (both virtues in Elizabethan eyes) becomes '*dull of tongue and dwarfish*', and the more Cleopatra crows her delight (relief), the more the terrified messenger warms to his theme now he knows what will please her. He gets his reward and Cleopatra swims onward, secure in the knowledge that she has nothing to fear in her rival.

In fact Octavia was one of history's unsung heroines: far from being the cold, passive pawn of Shakespeare's play, she was a remarkable woman, who bore Antony two children, the ancestors to three famous Roman emperors, Claudius, Caligula and Nero. She was often a political advisor to Antony and was called on to act as diplomatic go-between in the tricky relationship between Antony and her brother Octavius Caesar, and when Antony committed suicide, Octavia became the guardian of his and Cleopatra's children, taking them into her home and rearing them. But these facts would only muddy Shakespeare's dramatic purpose, which was to exonerate Antony for leaving his boring stick of a wife for the fascinating Cleopatra.

Enobarbus, in the most famous speech in the play, further exonerates his great leader by describing Antony's first sighting of Cleopatra in the famous barge of burnished gold whose sails were fanned by pretty cupids, etc., etc. By recreating the magic of the scene, Enobarbus implies that Rome's hero general was not weak, because no red-blooded man could have resisted Cleopatra's sorcery. Shakespeare took Enobarbus's description almost word for word from

Thomas North's translation of Plutarch, the Greek historian who became a Roman citizen. He was writing a hundred years after the events described and probably deliberately took an angle that was favourable to his adoptive country.

Once you know that Shakespeare is less concerned with historical accuracy or impartiality than he is with telling a very human story about exceptional people, everything falls into place.

In the play we never see the Cleopatra who is the extraordinary ruler of an Empire, speaker of several languages, expert in the sciences, astronomy and navigation. It is as though Shakespeare is not interested in all that, preferring the rather vain, ageing lover. That is more dramatically rich and ultimately poignant, and possibly far closer to his own heart.

I found this hard to stomach at times. A couple of scenes that had always stuck in my mind whenever I had seen the play, and which had put me off playing the part, concerned the preparation for the Battle of Actium and its aftermath. Shakespeare couches the whole ill-advised idea of doing battle by sea rather than land, in some petty game Cleopatra is playing in order to prove to Enobarbus that her influence on Antony is greater than his and can overcome all reasoned strategic wisdom. The real Cleopatra would never have sacrificed any possibility of victory for the sake of an increasingly fragile love affair. She would have anticipated the consequences that would not only be disastrous politically, but would also infect and eventually poison her relationship with Antony. The real Cleopatra saw that her ships, and all her wealth contained in them, would be trapped in the bay if she didn't escape immediately. It was a totally necessary and clever move, but in Shakespeare's play we have the wimpy, weeping Antony blaming his greatest defeat on his helplessness in face of the whims of his lover, who had just turned tail in mid-battle to test if he would follow or not.

O whither hast thou led me, Egypt?

Even her protestations—

> O my lord, my lord,
> Forgive my fearful sails! I little thought
> You would have follow'd

—are made to sound false by his

> Egypt, thou knew'st too well
> My heart was to thy rudder tied by the strings,
> And thou shouldst tow me after.

Here again, Shakespeare was not interested in telling the true story of the Battle of Actium. Instead he was fascinated by the codependency of two ageing, needy lovers.

Enobarbus

I am no academic. I don't create a character from the theories I develop from reading about them. It is the other way around, and that is what I find exciting. I put myself imaginatively and emotionally into a given dramatic scene, speak the words my character is given to speak, and, in the best cases, I learn something I could never have learnt through study. In this exercise of writing about a character long after I played her, I have tried to collect that experience into a coherent theory of the play. I enjoy exchanging these ideas with the learned Shakespearean scholars I have had the privilege to talk to, and it is great when we meet in the middle, both of us reaching some kind of understanding from our opposite starting points. One of the insights I arrived at purely through experiencing the performance was that Enobarbus and Cleopatra are a kind of mirror to one another. As I describe in Chapter Seven ('Two Loves'), both of them have a deep love for Antony and both can see—and hate to see—his decline. Enobarbus is more honest about what is happening, although he can only bring himself to describe it privately to the audience, while Cleopatra is in denial but behaves in ways that make it clear to Enobarbus that they are on the same page. Cleopatra knows that Enobarbus disapproves of her influence on Antony, but at the same time she is a woman who can make any man fall in love with her, and I think Enobarbus, despite himself, is no exception. Enobarbus understands Cleopatra better than Antony does, and explains her behaviour to the bewildered Antony. When Antony says, '*She is cunning past man's thought*', Enobarbus defends her:

> Alack, sir, no; her passions are made of nothing but the finest part of pure love.

And when Antony says, '*Would I had never seen her*', Enobarbus replies, '*O, sir, you had then left unseen a wonderful piece of work.*'

Enobarbus is our most reliable witness to both Antony and Cleopatra. He can see each more dispassionately than the other does, and he observes everything with the closeness of one who is deeply invested in both.

In Act III, Scene 13, Antony and Cleopatra are at a very low point. The scene begins with Antony offstage and Cleopatra asking, '*What shall we do, Enobarbus?*' This was a lovely, simple moment: it seems so familiar and right that a woman should ask her husband's best friend for help in dealing with her husband's flaws.

In our production, Antony then entered raging that Caesar has offered a deal with Cleopatra so long as she surrenders Antony to him. Cleopatra hears this for the first time, but in her tiny interjections into his rant we don't learn much about what she really feels. True love would never do such a deal, we think, but Cleopatra is partly in love with Antony's status, and to see him slighted this way, and reacting with irrational threats to take Caesar on in single combat, is a total turn-off. Enobarbus comments in the same vein to the audience but does not confide his thoughts to Cleopatra.

Cleopatra the hard-headed politician is now calculating her odds for survival, and, when she and Caesar's ambassador seem to be flirting and flattering one another, Enobarbus believes the worst and fetches Antony to witness the scene.

This is one of the most slippery and therefore most interesting scenes to play, because the actress can decide differently from night to night how far Cleopatra has fallen into temptation to buy her freedom by giving up Antony. Through Antony's jealous fit and his brutal whipping of Thyreus, Cleopatra has time to concoct an excuse, and the actress journeys with Cleopatra through disgust and guilt to some kind of pathos and reconciliation at the other side. This codependent pair feed one another's egos. Each sees themselves in the mirror of the other. They glory in each other's victories and hate the defeats. In defeat they start to loathe one another, but really it is their own failure that they are loathing. Cleopatra back-pedals furiously to set Antony back up on his pedestal, protesting far too much when he accuses her of being 'cold-hearted toward me'. Now she encourages him in all his ridiculous self-deceptive boasts ('That's my brave lord') and in an attempt to restore the enjoyment they used to have she tosses out the skittish line:

> It is my birthday.
> I had thought to have held it poor: but, since my lord
> Is Antony again, I will be Cleopatra.

The couple skip off the stage like teenagers, and the audience is left with very mixed emotions. They have watched the lovers dodge the test of their mutual trust. They had swerved to avoid the truth and patched things up superficially out of fear of losing one another. How totally human. It is left to Enobarbus to look truth in the face. He slopes off alone, and from here on, his path is one of isolation and eventual suicide.

The audience has come to rely on Enobarbus as the one sane voice in the insane story. As an actor waiting in the wings, I used to listen to his final speeches and became increasingly aware that Enobarbus is voicing the thoughts that Cleopatra dares not think.

A Rare Glimpse into Older Love

Of the Shakespeare plays I have been in, *Antony and Cleopatra, Macbeth* and *Hamlet* seem to show Shakespeare at his most psychologically modern and accurate. (Others will say this of *King Lear*, but I don't know that play so intimately.) Shakespeare's heroines are mostly young, and dominate the comedies, where the plots are all about young love, pursuit, rejection, and finally ending happily in marriage. Shakespeare then leaves us at that ending—which is actually a beginning—with no map as to how to continue.

In a sense I have grown up through Shakespeare. Not only have his demands on me as an actress forced me to mature and deepen, but he has taught me about life itself, offering me insights and providing me with words to describe so much of what I have felt. That is what makes it hard that he abandons women so early in their lives, and that is why I treasure my experience of playing Lady Macbeth and Cleopatra in particular because, through the actor's privilege of getting inside these characters rather than reading them on the page or watching them from outside, I can sense a link to the playwright himself perhaps examining his own middle-aged marriage through fully rounded, flawed, mature characters, both male and female. He seems to be speaking to me again. Beneath the exceptional dramatic circumstances of the plots of these two plays, we see the reality of a partnership with all its imperfections, its love/hate contradictions and its shifting power. That leads me to feel that these plays are Shakespeare's most personal plays and that *Antony and Cleopatra* is one of his most intimate plays, despite its public historical setting.

Act III, Scene 13 (mentioned above), felt like a major gear change in the relationship between Antony and Cleopatra. They have learnt a lot about one another rather suddenly. Their love has survived, but it has been deeply fractured and they are living on borrowed time. They are sobered in some way, and Cleopatra has more silences, more chances to question and observe this man who now often seems a stranger to her. The scenes themselves come thick and fast, darting between Egypt and Rome and back again. Scenes of extremely contrasting moods are juxtaposed for maximum nail-biting effect: a strange, maudlin Antony bids goodbye to his household on the eve of battle in Act IV, Scene 2, and once again Cleopatra has to ask Enobarbus what it all means. Antony then quickly covers it all up, pretending he didn't mean any of it and protesting '*I hope well of tomorrow*'. This is followed by a scene in which ordinary soldiers apprehensively wait for the day of battle to dawn. It is full of ominous sentences like '*Heard you nothing strange about the streets?*' and '*Have careful watch*'. Then one of them notices a strange sound of '*Music i' the air*' or was it '*under the earth*'? And all this is interpreted as '*the god Hercules, whom Antony loved, now leaves him*', reminding us of the semi-godlike reputation of the man we have seen up close and personal.

Then there is a playful scene where Cleopatra helps Antony into his armour, but there is a desperate sorrow behind her girlish laughter as she sends him off to war. So the plot races on with short scenes intercutting with a speed more appropriate to cinema than the stage. Shakespeare tosses us around between admiration of Antony (when we and Enobarbus learn of his generosity over Enobarbus's desertion), to horror at his misogyny (when he accuses Cleopatra of betraying him). Rather than face his own defeat, in soliloquy he blames the '*foul Egyptian*', the '*triple-turn'd whore!*' Cleopatra rushes to greet him and he turns his hatred on her:

Vanish, or I shall give thee thy deserving,
And blemish Caesar's triumph. Let him take thee,
And hoist thee up to the shouting plebeians:
Follow his chariot, like the greatest spot
Of all thy sex; most monster-like, be shown
For poor'st diminutives, for doits; and let
Patient Octavia plough thy visage up
With her prepared nails.

Patrick's Antony prepared to strike Cleopatra, and when she runs terrified away, Antony says, *'Tis well thou art gone.'* I found it so sad that this is actually the only scene where Antony and Cleopatra are alone on stage together and it is so brutal. The next time they speak to one another Antony is dying.

To the Monument

As in life, any ambivalence in a relationship evaporates at the approach of death. When Antony thinks (mistakenly) that Cleopatra is dead, he reaches for the most sublime poetry, putting all petty memories aside and enshrining their partnership back up there with the gods where they have always belonged.

I will o'ertake thee, Cleopatra… Stay for me:
Where souls do couch on flowers, we'll hand in hand,
And with our sprightly port make the ghosts gaze:
Dido and her Aeneas shall want troops,
And all the haunt be ours.

It got me every time as I listened up in the gods preparing to 'descend' into my monument on a narrow platform suspended above the stage that Greg and Stephen Brimson Lewis, the designer, had devised.

In the last rushed scene together, when Antony, who has even botched his suicide, learns that Cleopatra is not dead at all, and Cleopatra sees that her worst fears are being realised, and that their love risks a finale closer to farce than tragedy, the pair have their last gasp of earthly love. In another stroke of genius, Shakespeare offsets the highest-reaching poetry with the day-to-day banter of a marriage that is as familiar as a favourite cardy.

At one moment Cleopatra is commanding the elements to match the enormous scale of her feelings,

> O Sun,
> Burn the great sphere thou mov'st in!
> Darkling stand
> The varying shore o' the world!

—and the next moment she and Antony are squabbling childishly over who has the right to speak:

MARK ANTONY:
> I am dying, Egypt, dying:
> Give me some wine, and let me speak a little.

CLEOPATRA:
> No, let me speak; and let me rail so high,
> That the false housewife Fortune break her wheel,
> Provoked by my offence.

MARK ANTONY:
> One word, sweet queen…

(*CLEOPATRA:*
> …*Oh, okay…*)

and he continues.

When Antony is dead, Cleopatra has some of the most electrifying and emotional lines any character ever spoke. The lines speak to all of us when we are high on grief. We do not have to have been married to an emperor or a hero for these lines to drop to the centre of our hearts:

> Noblest of men, woo't die?
> Hast thou no care of me? shall I abide
> In this dull world, which in thy absence is
> No better than a sty? O, see, my women,

(MARK ANTONY *dies.*)

> The crown o' the earth doth melt. My lord!
> O, wither'd is the garland of the war,
> The soldier's pole is fall'n: young boys and girls
> Are level now with men; the odds is gone,
> And there is nothing left remarkable
> Beneath the visiting moon.

I played out these scenes eighteen months after my own partner had died, and what a therapeutic gift it was to have such poetry in my head and my heart every night.

In the next passage, Shakespeare contrasts the woman with the gods, encapsulating the interior split in personality which Cleopatra herself experiences:

> No more, but e'en a woman, and commanded
> By such poor passion as the maid that milks
> And does the meanest chares. It were for me
> To throw my sceptre at the injurious gods;
> To tell them that this world did equal theirs
> Till they had stol'n our jewel.

Her ferocity and helplessness are regal and human at the same time, and her '*infinite variety*' is demonstrated in the way in which she switches from the simplest, most beautiful bonding with her women:

> Ah, women, women, look,
> Our lamp is spent, it's out!

to a rather hearty practicality:

> Good sirs, take heart: We'll bury him;

to the soldier/priestess inspiring her followers:

> and then what's brave, what's noble,
> Let's do it after the high Roman fashion,
> And make death proud to take us.

Then comes an attempt at objectivity:

> Come, away:
> This case of that huge spirit now is cold,

which is suddenly overtaken by a relapse into grief:

> Ah, women, women!

Then a revival and deepened resolve:

> come; we have no friend
> But resolution, and the briefest end.

Over to You, Cleo

So now it is Act V, and it's over to you, the actor playing
Cleopatra. You walk on to the dimly lit stage, a drab shadow of
your former self. Your devoted women wait to hear your bid-
ding. You have already told the audience that there is '*nothing
left remarkable / Beneath the visiting moon*' and that you have
no wish to stay in '*this dull world*'. Now you must hold the
stage, and shoulder the memory of Antony for the entire final
act with no showy sets, costumes or tricks to help you.

Stripped of glory and drained of emotion, a deadly clarity
comes to you, and with that clarity a calm and light that we
have not seen in Cleopatra and that she has not seen in herself. I found I could say these lines as though each thought
were totally new to her/me:

> My desolation does begin to make
> A better life. 'Tis paltry to be Caesar;
> Not being Fortune, he's but Fortune's knave,
> A minister of her will: and it is great
> To do that thing that ends all other deeds;
> Which shackles accidents and bolts up change;
> Which sleeps, and never palates more the dung,
> The beggar's nurse and Caesar's.

Her own surprising thoughts give her courage. Shakespeare
has created a character who is a brilliant actress, always aware
of her audience and capable of acting out nobility. Perhaps

now these qualities can *truly* be found deep within her. This is the test for the actor playing her. I am an unremarkable woman playing a very remarkable one. I *pretend* for a living, but to do real justice to myself, my profession and perhaps to Cleopatra, I must now do more than pretend. This act, which reveals a new self-honesty in Cleopatra, demands the utmost honesty from me. We must go beyond show and tricks into some deeper internal territory, the well-spring for true and less demonstrated emotions.

At the top of the act I know this is where I must aim, but there is still some way to go. Cleopatra will rally all her personae in order to survive the many traps that Caesar has laid for her. Before the act is out we will see the feral fighter with Caesar's soldiers; the seductress with Dolabella and with Caesar himself; the trickster with Seleucus her treasurer; then, as we get closer to the heart of her, we see the motherly mistress to her handmaidens; the joker with the Clown who brings the asp in a basket of figs; and then she builds back up to the most theatrical moment of her life, her monumental death and ultimate victory against Caesar.

Some years ago I was asked to give a masterclass on *Antony and Cleopatra* to some American drama students. I don't know what they learnt from it but I learnt something I didn't know I knew, or at least had never articulated.

One of the students was asked to deliver Cleopatra's famous eulogy on Antony:

> I dream'd there was an Emperor Antony:
> O, such another sleep, that I might see
> But such another man! [etc., etc.]

It is one of the greatest speeches I have ever had the luxury of speaking, but there lies the rub. One must not luxuriate in it. The student was delivering the speech so engulfed in her own luxurious misery that the words were indecipherable. All an audience could see was: 'That woman is very unhappy about something.' I too had loved the luxury of the speech, but I also knew that more important than my feelings were the words and the images that I/Cleopatra had to sell to the audience *and* of course, to Dolabella, who will take the message back to Caesar.

Dolabella is the Roman soldier that Caesar sends to seduce Cleopatra into accepting the offer of living captivity rather than glorious death. Cleopatra's desperation sharpens all her powers, and it is she who ends up seducing Dolabella with the depth of her feeling. I told the drama student that every line of the speech was designed as a weapon or a political tool. The speech was a eulogy, yes, but it was also blatant propaganda, the message being: 'You think you and your paltry emperor are so great? I will show you what a real emperor is. You little bureaucrats are nothing to me, and what's more, I may not look much now, but any woman loved by that extraordinary giant is not to be messed with, and will not be impressed by your guy.'

As you speak those lines and reach so far out for those images, Shakespeare's music does work on you and raw emotions do well up and threaten to choke you, but the words *have* to cut through all that. It is the words that will affect the audience, and the actor should keep their own feelings in check enough to make the speech active and not a passive rumination or self-indulgence. That is what I told the student, but I was teaching myself as well.

In Act V we see Cleopatra the practised politician: the woman who has been dodging plots against her life since childhood. She knows she has a way out via suicide, and now she can play her last game to the hilt.

She knows that her suicide will damage Caesar's reputation and add to her own mythology. That is her one weapon. Caesar wants no tragic martyr. He wants Cleopatra alive and conquered and paraded through the streets of Rome. First she tries to bargain with Caesar's emissary, Proculeius, to secure Egypt for her son. She asks for Caesar himself to meet with her face to face. Maybe she can still muster her old powers to dazzle and distract him. In our production John Hopkins, who played Caesar, entered the monument with his hands shielding his eyes from the sight of Cleopatra. He knew of her reputation and was determined not to fall under her spell.

Cleopatra should be so convincing in her seeming contrition and gratitude to Caesar for his offer of a lifeline that the audience almost believe, with him, that he has won her over. But immediately after he and his entourage have cleared the stage, she blurts out:

> He words me, girls, he words me, that I should not
> Be noble to myself,

as if to say, 'I fooled him, but he can't fool me.'

Her courage and certitude are building up to her suicide, step by inexorable step. Her more 'normal' fearful handmaidens need comforting and inspiring, something she has the insight and tenderness to do. Then, in one of the most extraordinary moments for me, in her only (very short) soliloquy in the play, she privately notices:

> My resolution's placed, and I have nothing
> Of woman in me: now from head to foot
> I am marble-constant; now the fleeting moon
> No planet is of mine.

Shakespeare often puts the word 'woman' or 'womanish tears' into the mouths of his characters as a taunt or an insult. It was deep within the culture of his time that to give in to feelings was female and weak and that the moon was inconstant and unreliable, like women. Shakespeare seems to subscribe to that theory and to perpetuate it. The fact that he often demonstrates the opposite in action makes me wonder what he really felt.

The ever-confounding Shakespeare introduces a comic clown just when we are preparing for the high-point of tragedy. The Clown presents Cleopatra with the asp that he has managed to smuggle past the guards. The scene is not exactly hilarious, but it is strange and wonderful. Cleopatra and the Clown seem to understand one another, fellow actors in a story. He speaks cryptically of '*the worm*', but we know that he knows what she is about to do with it, and in his parting shot, '*I wish you joy of the worm*', we hear Death itself as a friend and co-conspirator.

Now we are truly alone again. Just we three women. Let us get on with it. There is no time to lose. Caesar will be back soon, and we must prepare the final triumphant victory image that will crush him and give me immortality. Come, my stage managers and my dressers. Hurry up: I am long-ing with all my heart to meet Antony again. He is waiting for me. He will approve of this. I am a true Egyptian, and I know there is an afterlife. I have settled my future and my country's future.

> Give me my robe, put on my crown.

There is an urgency and an excitement to Cleopatra's last speeches that cuts against any monumental gravitas or sad-ness, although after her death it is precisely gravitas and sadness that affect the remaining players who wind up the play.

Having wrestled with a snake (sometimes a real one, some-times a fake: we tried both), I lie there on my throne with my eyes shut, listening to Caesar's closing speech:

> Take up her bed;
> And bear her women from the monument:
> She shall be buried by her Antony:
> No grave upon the earth shall clip in it
> A pair so famous.

I imagine Cleopatra can hear him too and is smiling at her triumph, and that even though I may not have matched her grandeur, at least I am no squeaking boy.

BRUTUS
The Honorary Man

As Brutus
Julius Caesar, Donmar Warehouse, 2012

In 2012 I started on what has become a four-year, three-play, all-female Shakespeare project with the director Phyllida Lloyd and the Donmar Warehouse. This, and the following chapter, are written in the midst of it. After playing the first part of this trilogy, Julius Caesar, *at the Donmar in 2012, we took it to St Ann's Warehouse in Brooklyn in 2013.*

> It sometimes takes a woman to show us what men are truly made of. Just as a skilled drag queen reminds us of the artifice that shapes our images of femininity, women portraying macho men highlight what's grotesque and confining in traditionally masculine postures.
>
> Ben Brantley, *New York Times*

Who is Entitled?

Where do you go after Cleopatra's magnificent death? Alright, there is Volumnia, or the Countess of Rousillon; Paulina is a possible, and there's mad Margaret; but that is pretty well it, and none of them has the infinite variety of the Egyptian Queen.

Playing Cleopatra, I had learnt new lessons and reached new heights—or plateaux—from which I could see a further range above me that I hadn't known was there, but those lessons looked like they would never be put into practice and those further peaks would remain on the horizon never to be scaled.

Then along came Phyllida Lloyd and her idea of an all-female Shakespeare season at the Donmar Warehouse. It was not a new idea. A handful of women have played male roles in every century since Shakespeare died. Nor was it the first time anyone had talked to me about playing a male role in Shakespeare, but things had remained at the talking stage.

Phyllida caught me at a time when I had accepted that my Shakespeare days were over. I was lucky to keep busy with other work on stage and screen, but there was always that low background hum of longing for Shakespeare. To be barred from speaking those words, from that lung-filling, mind-altering, self-testing practice, was like being a concert pianist forbidden to open the lid of the piano.

As Phyllida's idea took deeper root, we overcame our initial doubts and became sure that there was something a group of women could say by performing these male plays.

The classics are revisited for what they can tell us about our world today, and the world today is much more feminised than in Shakespeare's lifetime. Women, in the West at least, have access to perform in any and every field of public endeavour, in theory at least. Could we not play the male leaders in our national playwright's canon? And if it looked or felt wrong, wouldn't we have to ask ourselves useful questions as to why? We are continually broadening the definition of what a man or a woman is, so couldn't we be holding Shakespeare's mirror up to the nature of a more current world?

The problem to me had always been permission: permission from the public and permission from myself. I may have wanted to keep in the Shakespeare game, but if that meant playing men, the public didn't need to watch me do it. This was why I had never taken the idea further than speculation. I needed Phyllida's nerve and thereby *her* permission. What could I as a performer bring to any male role that a male could not do better? Would it not just be a vanity exercise?

Then I thought, hey! What male actor do I know who would not jump at playing Hamlet for the sake of playing Hamlet, never mind that the world arguably does not need another one for a decade? The public will go to these productions in search of the latest bearer of the 'Great Actor' baton from Richard Burbage, through Garrick, Kean, Irving, Gielgud, David Warner, Jonathan Pryce, Mark Rylance, Ben Whishaw, and on and on, all in their way personifying the hero or anti-hero of our age. There is no questioning any male actor's right to take up the torch. But what right have I…?

In my very coyness lurked a revelation. I had a typically female attitude. I didn't feel entitled. We women can be as ambitious as men and as hungry, but then that old chestnut of needing to be liked rears its head. It sounds daft but it is a not-to-be-ignored factor that contributes to women's ongoing underachievement in the top echelons of public life. A woman CEO or police commander or politician not only has to do a demanding job but in addition she must be armed against a mass of prejudice and personal dislike that will inevitably come her way. You only have to look at the vile, personal, sexist attacks in the media during Hillary Clinton's election campaigns in 2008 and 2016, to see that irrational antagonism against a woman is somehow deemed an acceptable form of public discussion. The equivalent racism against Barack Obama had to be more carefully disguised. A large number of women have decided that this kind of institutional misogyny is too high a price to pay for doing a tough job and prefer to balance career achievements with social acceptability and family life.

But I am only an actor. Could I not risk a bit of criticism from my male colleagues and male critics? Of course I bloody could. So I put off worrying about such things till opening night and committed myself to the journey with Phyllida.

We wondered which play to pick. On Phyllida's shortlist were *Romeo and Juliet*, *Julius Caesar* and *Hamlet*. *Julius Caesar* won almost because it was the least obvious for women to play. Love is the customary territory for Shakespeare's women, and *Hamlet* is a bit of a solo act. *Julius Caesar* is about power, the struggle for it, the gaining of it and how to use it when you have it. The prospect of women playing out that story from inside male characters quickly excited me.

We talked much of how to 'justify' an all-female *Julius Caesar*, and one day Phyllida came in with the idea of setting the play in a female prison. The advantages of this were that we would be de-sexed by our uniform, it would explain why there were no male actors, the violence and aggression in the play would be more convincing in a prison context, and it is no stretch to imagine prisoners playing Shakespeare as it is now a fairly common practice for actors to do workshops in prisons.

By coincidence I had just been performing a scene from *King Lear* with a young Serbian prisoner in a correction centre in Malta with Bruce Wall's London Shakespeare Workout, and my loose connection with his wonderful group had familiarised me with the benefits of prisoners playing Shakespeare. I knew there were many such groups doing wonderful things, giving voices to the most forgotten people and confidence to people of rock-bottom self-esteem. The work does not wave a Pollyanna wand, but it does leave people changed in their view of themselves as individuals and it welcomes them in as participants in a shared story of humanity. So Phyllida's idea seemed not only to be totally grounded in possibility, but also provided a perfect metaphor for the way women's voices are largely excluded from the centre of our cultural history.

I wasn't sure at first which part I wanted to play. It never having been a possibility, I had never thought about playing Brutus, but after a bit of discussion I agreed to play him. So how would the rest of the cast be picked? There are enough experienced, talented female actors of my age group and younger to cast the play six times over, but once the prison idea had established itself, we needed a cast that could believably represent the racial and social mix of a prison population. This prerequisite sent the casting net far wider than the typical RSC or Globe or National Theatre lists, so during the auditioning process I met female performers from all backgrounds, disciplines and degrees of experience, and I was privy to some wonderfully creative discussions between Phyllida and the Donmar's casting genius, Anne McNulty.

To add into the mix, I had long been a patron of Clean Break, a theatre company set up by two women, while they themselves were in prison, to explore the inmates' lives and prison issues through drama and which went on to develop into the producing/training/commissioning powerhouse it is now. I suggested that we might collaborate with them in some way, and so the Donmar hired some Clean Break actors, who brought a completely fresh tone to Shakespeare and at the same time provided us with invaluable first-hand knowledge of prison life to make the setting feel as authentic as possible.

If a white, middle-class, educated Shakespeare pro like me felt a lack of entitlement, how must a young black woman from South London who had never spoken a word of Shakespeare feel? I discovered that one or two of the very youngest members of the cast had a sort of 'What's the problem?' attitude which I found very hopeful. It seemed that their generation were already blurring the edges between genders, classes and race and had not bought into the cultural segregation that the older ones had grown up with. One of the most rewarding outcomes of the whole adventure was to watch various company members grow in confidence and ability before my eyes. It was humbling to realise that the audience felt no distinction between my achievement, building on my whole Shakespearean career, and that of a first-time player. What rocked them was the total commitment, clarity and energy they got off each and every one of us. None of us took this privilege for granted as perhaps some male actors might do. We were all contributing wholeheartedly to creating a believable world, and the audience willingly suspended their disbelief. If any one of us had dropped the ball, we would have shattered the whole illusion, and I, for one, would have felt a total fraud.

Brutus and 'Hannah'

In preparation for rehearsals, Phyllida and I visited a group of women in Holloway Prison and did some workshops with them. It was a frustratingly short interlude, and the prison agenda tended to marginalise our work, changing the attendees of the group at the last minute, whisking people out to take their 'meds', shunting us from one un-atmospheric room to another. On one occasion, while our group were passionately acting out the murder of Caesar, someone bashed into the room and started energetically working a floor-polisher under and around our feet with a disregard for what we were doing that was so astonishing as to inspire a brief interlude in the final production.

From the Holloway women we did get confirmation that the play was the right one to do. The themes of violence, loyalty, competition, suicide, and the marginalised quality of the domestic scenes all resonated with them. We were also encouraged by how speedily they had grasped the meaning of the text, and, in one case at least, we saw a budding natural talent for verse speaking.

When the cast met for rehearsals we watched some TV documentaries about British women's prisons and noticed how so many women aped male behaviour and played out relationships with one another that mirrored the male/female relationships they experienced on the outside. There were many self-harmers (a link to Portia's desperate act of wounding herself in the thigh), but there was also a lot of humour and paradoxically a lot of tenderness. All of these qualities could be used in our play.

For me the elephant in the room was: 'What would a person like Harriet Walter be doing in a prison?' Most women in prison in this country shouldn't be there. A tiny percentage have committed violent acts. Nearly all of their crimes are petty and a huge percentage are drug-related. An even more interesting statistic is that nearly all women in jail are there because of a man in their life: a pimp, a drug dealer, or a violent partner. I came from a privileged, enlightened background and what I most feared was having to 'pretend' too much. I already needed to suspend people's disbelief by playing a Roman general, but on top of that I needed people to believe in a prisoner who could act fluently in Shakespeare's language.

Phyllida had encouraged each of us to invent a prison character who in some way matched our Shakespeare character. To make any other choice would be unproductive. One of our Clean Break members helped us rank our characters in a prison hierarchy, for such a thing exists, whereby some crimes are more respected than others. Thus the actress playing Cinna the Poet, who is violently beaten up by the mob, chose to be in for a hit-and-run car accident, a low status, much despised crime, which upped the ante in the fight which got out of hand and tipped over into something rather too real (but of course *not* real).

So who would my character be? My little acting mantra that I use in the wings or when first approaching a character is 'This could be me'. If I were not born into my circumstances at my time into this body, I could be any other human being. It is the actor's version of time travel. So, given that social advantages and education reduce the likelihood of committing crimes, why might someone like me land up in prison? Driving offences? Sure. Some kind of tax fraud? Quite possible. Manslaughter? Not impossible. But none of these matched Brutus.

My Clean Break friend told us how someone with education would command immediate respect, not necessarily affection but a recognition of potential authority. That respect could be built on or lost depending on how that prisoner continued to behave. I needed to find a prison character who wanted to put her education to helpful use, someone who had earned respect over a period of time, so probably serving a long sentence. Someone who, like Brutus, passionately and genuinely cared about the principle of democracy, who needed to expiate a past guilt and believed in redemption. She was beginning to shape up into a political prisoner, a revolutionary who in her youth had rebelled against the system of privilege that had formed her. I was the right generation for this kind of profile, but Britain did not have any political prisoners, now that the IRA have been released. How about Baader-Meinhof? Patty Hearst? All too specific geographically. Nevertheless, I followed this idea through, and, given that our stage prison was not supposed to mirror any particular factual prison, I created Hannah.

Hannah was a combination of people I had read about, in particular one: Judith Clark, an American prisoner jailed for life for her involvement in a bank robbery conducted by an anti-capitalist revolutionary group in the early 1980s. Three people died as a result of the raid, and although Clark was only the getaway driver, through a combination of being in the wrong place at the wrong time and extreme non-cooperation (she refused to attend her own trial in protest against the entire legal system), she received a longer sentence (life without parole) than the rest of the gang, even than the trigger-pullers. She is a mother and a grandmother and has had to face her own terrible feelings of guilt for the life she has led her family into. When I read about this woman it was in a fairly recent article describing her complete turnaround over her years in jail. A story so profound that I cannot even begin it here. Suffice to say, I could latch on to her as a real person to feed into my speculative creation, Hannah.

Hannah/Judith could be me. Hannah would become a mentor figure to the other women, a teacher with a missionary zeal to equip them with an education and skills with which to improve their lives. Hannah might well have learnt her Shakespeare by joining one of Bruce Wall's visiting groups, and she might have earned enough trust from the prison staff to be charged with helping to put on a play and passing on her skills. She would definitely have seen *Julius Caesar* as a perfect vehicle in which to play out her own inner debates, and she would care desperately about getting it right. The production would be the be-all-and-end-all of her otherwise barren prison days.

Hannah/Judith was a far more extreme politico than I had ever been and is now a far more profound and brave woman than I expect ever to be. I would have to reach for her just as I have to reach beyond myself to the noble Brutus.

So Who is Brutus?

He is a patrician from an ancient Roman family. He is part of the establishment and has the ear of Caesar. He has recently fought against Caesar in the war with Pompey, a fact that Caesar seems to have forgiven. His wife Portia is the daughter of Cato, himself no lover of Caesar's; but I won't embark on the inter-familial entanglements of the Roman world. It is enough to know that Brutus is conflicted. He is

also the most universally respected man of the moment.
Cinna, one of the conspirators against Caesar, shows us a
hint of Brutus's particular importance to their cause:

> O Cassius, if you could
> But win the noble Brutus to our party—

tailing off because it seems an impossible dream as Brutus
is so close to Caesar.

Cassius is the most purely revolutionary character in the
play. He is not hampered by love of Caesar as Brutus is. He
is clear-eyed about the situation, saying:

> Caesar doth bear me hard; but he loves Brutus.

He knows that Brutus has more to lose, but precisely
because he is seen by the people to be respected by Caesar,
Brutus will have a vital role to play as unifier after Caesar's
assassination. He is the key man. The conspirators cannot
act without him.

In his opening scene with Brutus we see Cassius avidly
searching Brutus's face for clues to his thoughts and ready
to pounce on Brutus's verbal hesitations as signs of a chink
in his armour. He knows he can play on Brutus's genuine
passion for republicanism and his hatred of Caesar's increasingly despotic regime. By the end of the scene he can say:

> Well, Brutus, thou art noble; yet, I see,
> Thy honourable metal may be wrought
> From that it is disposed.

A little further tipping (by way of some anonymous notes),
and Brutus is won over to the cause. Cassius has worked on
Brutus rather as Lady Macbeth works on her husband.
Cassius knows Brutus's heart and prods his deeper ambition
into action. As Hamlet says: '*Conscience doth make cowards
of us all*', but once Brutus has wrestled with his conscience,
he rushes to the forefront of the fight and puts his doubts
behind him. For a while…

I had never realised what a complex and interesting character Brutus is. In the Shakespeare panoply he is related to both Hamlet and Macbeth, almost as mentally tortured as the former, almost as guilt-ridden as the latter, but not as self-explicit as either. It made his soliloquies quite tantalising. He is a private man who can't even open up to his best friend, Cassius:

> Vexed I am
> Of late with passions of some difference,
> Conceptions only proper to myself.

Even when he does privately talk to the audience he is oblique, and this seems to indicate that he is not even sure what he himself thinks, or is it that he is not 100 per cent honest with himself, unable to look his own ambition and darker tendencies straight in the eye?

All this made his first soliloquy extremely tricky. I thought I knew what he was feeling, but he never quite expressed it, and it was therefore almost impossible to convey to the audience. I even wondered if it was a speech that Shakespeare had written for another play and had it knocking around in a bottom drawer waiting to slot it in somewhere, so inappropriate was some of it to the situation.

For a start, by the time he was assassinated, Caesar had already destroyed the whole notion of Republicanism. He had abolished elections, limited the powers of the law courts, stopped free speech... the list goes on. So Rome was already a dictatorship. But Brutus keeps referring to a *potential* dictatorship that might arise if nothing is done to stop it. He says Caesar 'may *do danger*' (my emphasis), and that '*lowliness is young ambition's ladder*'. What has that got to do with the well-established fifty-six-year-old Caesar? Following through with the ladder metaphor, he talks of people pulling the ladder up behind them, '*so Caesar* may' and, '*lest he may, prevent*'.

Another metaphor he uses is that of letting loose '*the adder... that craves wary walking*', and he resolves to think of Caesar '*as a serpent's egg / Which, hatch'd, would, as his kind, grow mischievous*', and so best to '*kill him in the shell*'.

None of these reasons is strong enough to justify murder. You don't kill someone because they *might* become a monster. A man like Brutus could never be persuaded to assassinate a leader and a friend unless things had reached a point of no return, but Shakespeare robbed him (and me) of the most powerful arguments.

The one thing I could seize on was the imminent danger that Caesar is to be crowned King the next day. It is hard to convey to a modern audience the dread that the word 'King' held for the Romans. Caesar as King would be worse even than Caesar the dictator, because kings form dynasties. Their unelected sons become kings after them, and inherited power was the antithesis of Republicanism. Once the crown was on Caesar's head there would be no going back. It must be now and '*It must be by his death*'.

Out of my frustration at Brutus's equivocation I discovered that that was the point. Shakespeare was interested in a man '*with himself at war*'. He wanted to show a man of conscience, a decent man, one whom we would quite like to take over the country, searching his heart and trying to stoke himself up to a terrible act by way of some pretty spurious arguments. So I reconciled myself to the fact that the speech tells us more about Brutus than about what is really happening.

'Brutus is an honourable man'...

...is almost an advertising slogan that Brutus himself has bought into. The number of times he refers to his own honour seems to protest a little too much. Cynics say that is because he is as nakedly ambitious as the next man but won't admit it to himself, but I am not a cynic and I don't believe Shakespeare wants to tell that particular story about the hero/anti-hero of the play. I think Brutus is certainly not without ambition and fears it in himself. He frequently re-states the slogan of his honour because he wants to live up to his ideal and needs a reminder to keep himself on track. He sees with clarity that

> The abuse of greatness is, when it disjoins
> Remorse from power.

He wants to believe that moral integrity and leadership can coexist so he strives to become the change he wants to see in the world. Being a cynical, power-hungry villain is easy by comparison.

Brutus so desperately needs to think himself honourable that he has to disguise murder as something more accept-able to his conscience. To the conspirators he advocates carving Caesar's body as '*a dish fit for the gods*'. He so needs the world to think him honourable that he gives a tutorial on how to spin a word (my emphasis):

> Let us be sacrificers, but not butchers...
> Which so *appearing* to the common eyes,
> We shall be call'd purgers, not murderers.

This same need informs his argument against killing Mark Antony:

> Our course will *seem* too bloody.

He is also no stranger to duplicity, urging the conspirators to go to the Capitol looking '*fresh and merrily*':

> Let not our looks put on our purposes,
> But bear it as our Roman actors do.

It is hard, within the body of the text, to find any proof of love between Brutus and Caesar. Shakespeare doesn't give them a scene together or any other chance to demonstrate it. The only clues are in Brutus's protestations to Cassius of his love for Caesar, and Caesar's enshrined dying words, '*Et tu, Brute*', designed to bed themselves into Brutus's conscience forever. In our 2012 version Caesar was played as a monstrous manipulator punishing or petting in equal, unpredictable measure. The prison character was called Frankie, and her prison identity was ambiguous. Some saw her as alpha bitch, some as top prison rebel, in and out of solitary, some as mother/father figure. Her true identity would be revealed in the last seconds of the play.

Whoever she was, it was clear that she had top status, with Brutus/Hannah close behind. We decided that she had directed the play, and this accounted for her continuing watchful presence long after Caesar's death, just as the ghost of Caesar hovers over Shakespeare's play.

At the point of doing the bloody deed, all Brutus's protective words desert him. Murder is murder. He will find it harder to believe in his own honour from now on. In contrast to Macbeth, whose first treacherous act tips him down an irreversible slide to evil, Brutus just becomes more and more desperate for a good end to justify the means.

I often thought of Barack Obama—that rare creature: a morally intelligent leader—and how some of his well-intentioned decisions have not always been the best political ones. When Brutus argues against Cassius's idea of killing Mark Antony as well as Caesar, and when, later, he gives Mark Antony permission to speak at Caesar's funeral, he inadvertently sets in motion the destruction of everything he and his co-conspirators have fought for. He hopes that allowing Mark Antony to live and to speak will demonstrate to the world that theirs will be a reasonable and transparent government. Cassius is the shrewder, less trusting politician; and the play tragically proves him right.

Brutus also misjudges the crowd when he has his chance to justify the assassination. The real Brutus was a lawyer, and Shakespeare gives him all the advantages of a great legal orator. If we look at the following speech, we find the rule of three frequently used for climactic effect. We see antithetical slogans with plenty of good soundbites for memorising:

> Not that I loved Caesar less, but that I loved Rome more,

and

> Had you rather Caesar were living and die all slaves, than
> that Caesar were dead, to live all free men?

We see the neat pay-off of word set against word, and in particular his own buzz-word, 'honour', which he can assume the crowd attaches to him:

> believe me for mine honour, and have respect to mine
> honour, that you may believe.

He offers them his own tears for his friend, but hatred for Caesar's '*ambition*' (which I found a totally unhelpful understatement with which to put my case)—and in the speech below I have marked how he breaks out of the rule of three to add a fourth by way of emphasising how Caesar's ambition oversteps the bounds.

Finally he uses a rhetorical structure to emotionally blackmail any disbelievers into buttoning their lips and joining the cause.

> Romans (1), countrymen (2), and lovers (3)!

> Hear me for my cause, and be silent, that you may hear (1):
> believe me for mine honour, and have respect to mine
> honour, that you may believe (2): censure me in your
> wisdom, and awake your senses, that you may the better
> judge (3).

> If there be any in this assembly, any dear friend of
> Caesar's, to him I say, that Brutus' love to Caesar was no
> less than his. If then that friend demand why Brutus rose
> against Caesar, this is my answer:

> —Not that I loved Caesar less, but that I loved Rome
> more.

> Had you rather Caesar were living and die all slaves, than
> that Caesar were dead, to live all free men?

> As Caesar loved me, I weep for him (1); as he was
> fortunate, I rejoice at it (2); as he was valiant, I honour

him (3): but, as he was ambitious, I slew him (4). There is tears for his love (1); joy for his fortune (2); honour for his valour (3); and death for his ambition (4).

Who is here so base that would be a bondman? If any, speak; for him have I offended (1).

Who is here so rude that would not be a Roman? If any, speak; for him have I offended (2). Who is here so vile that will not love his country? If any, speak; for him have I offended (3). I pause for a reply...

Then none have I offended.

It is a brilliant speech, but not brilliant enough.

The crowd are won over, but Mark Antony wins them back by hitting so many more of the people's buttons than Brutus ever could. The revolution against Caesar was essentially an upper-class revolution and so failed to get the people behind it. The upper class were more or less under house arrest, and, being close to power, they keenly felt the lack of it. By contrast, Caesar had been clever enough to keep the lower classes relatively well fed and content. The conspirators' mistake was in not recognising that these people bore Caesar no grudge, and even loved him. Mark Antony was able to play on this and kick the country into civil war.

Men Don't Cry

Masculinity is a carapace that protects men in battle: hard but inflexible, strong yet brittle. It permits no expression of feelings, doubt or weakness.

Grayson Perry

When we had asked the female prisoners in Holloway what they thought women could bring to *Julius Caesar* that men wouldn't, several answered 'emotion'.

We next see Brutus at the height of the war. His feelings are raw. He may have killed his leader only to supplant him with an even worse order. The only way he can live with this thought is to believe his way of honour can win. It must. Then he learns that his closest ally Cassius has been sanctioning bribes, and the two men have a stormy row in Brutus's tent.

This is the most brilliant scene in the play, and the fact that it was acted by women gave it a double life. On the one hand two men, whose brotherly bond only soldiers can know; on the other two women shouting at one another, physically threatening and pushing each other. Physical closeness has very different connotations for men and women, as does overt aggression—something females practically never show in friendship and certainly would not easily recover from in the way that Brutus and Cassius do.

We actresses focused on each of our character's passionate views. Brutus/Hannah is full of idealistic anger:

> shall we now
> Contaminate our fingers with base bribes,
> And sell the mighty space of our large honours?

Cassius (prisoner name: Noma) lashes out in defence of pragmatism:

> In such a time as this it is not meet
> That every nice offence should bear his comment.

Women actors brought out the school playground nature of the male posturing…

CASSIUS:
> I am a soldier, I,
> Older in practice, abler than yourself
> To make conditions.

BRUTUS:
> Go to; you are not, Cassius.

CASSIUS:
> I am.

BRUTUS:
> I say you are not…

CASSIUS:
> ...I said, an elder soldier, not a better:
> Did I say 'better'?

BRUTUS:
> If you did, I care not.

But it also showed how emotionally entangled these warrior men are. The following extract reminds one of a marital row.

CASSIUS:
> You love me not.

BRUTUS:
> I do not like your faults.

CASSIUS:
> A friendly eye could never see such faults.

BRUTUS:
> A flatterer's would not, though they do appear
> As huge as high Olympus.

It culminates in a great histrionic demonstration by Cassius and a threat of suicide—

> There is my dagger,
> And here my naked breast...
> Strike, as thou didst at Caesar; for, I know,
> When thou didst hate him worst, thou lovedst him better
> Than ever thou lovedst Cassius

—proving that men *do* use emotional blackmail in their arguments just as they accuse women of doing.

It has the right effect. Cassius's alter-ego, Noma, had been a self-harmer. For any audience close enough to see, she had a criss-cross of scarring all up her arms. Hannah rushes in to take the knife off her (or the sharpened toothbrush handle as used in prisons) and rocks her in her arms. This action matches the men's tender words. Brutus is about to reveal that Portia has just committed suicide in despair at how the war is turning out. To also have the blood of his closest friend on his hands would have been too much to bear.

The audience don't need to know of all these layers beneath the scene. In fact they shouldn't know. Shakespeare drops the bombshell of Portia's death simply and quietly after the row has died down. It may retrospectively explain Brutus's fierceness, but Shakespeare deliberately delays our feelings of sympathy for Brutus.

Phyllida further delayed the audience's sympathy by staging a 'breakout' moment (as we called them). In the tiny turnaround time between the end of the row and Brutus's announcement of Portia's death, some of the inmates started giggling and talking loudly outside 'the tent'. Hannah was so 200 per cent engaged in the project for all her own personal reasons and this was such a highly charged moment in the play that I/Hannah broke out of character, rushed up to the disruptors and blasted them with something different every night depending on my whim. It was deliberately inappropriate and startling. I won't analyse the effect on the audience because I am not entirely sure what it was, but it shifted the ground and upped the stakes and reminded people that a theatre can be an unsafe and unpredictable place. Was that Brutus? A prisoner? or Harriet Walter losing the plot?

I am not sure whether the incident helped or hindered me in getting back to Brutus's grief as he tells Cassius of Portia's death. It was a wonderful moment to play. This simple line coming from left field during their conversation: '*Portia is dead.*'

Cassius is stopped in his tracks: '*Ha! Portia!*'

Brutus repeats, '*She is dead.*'

It is stated unhistrionically. Then Brutus gives way to tears but very abruptly cuts off with '*Speak no more of her. Give me a bowl of wine.*' Back to business. Where are the generals? Come in, chaps. Let's talk strategy. But then Shakespeare does this extraordinary thing, and, as often happens, something puzzling in the text forces up an interesting discovery. General Messala asks Brutus whether he has heard any news of his wife. Brutus says no. Is this a mistake? Was this scene written earlier than the one before and Shakespeare had forgotten to edit it out? What is this about?

The general hums and haws, and Brutus says, 'Out with it': '*As you are a Roman tell me true.*' The general then tells him Portia is dead, and Brutus reacts in the strangest way:

> Why, farewell, Portia. We must die, Messala:
> With meditating that she must die once,
> I have the patience to endure it now.

And then I understood. Messala's next words are:

> Even so great men great losses should endure.

Brutus has used the moment to demonstrate to his men a patrician self-restraint that we know is not the whole picture. It rings bells even now when men are trained not to cry and certainly not in public. Tears cloud the judgment and leaders need to be clear.

As a woman playing the part of a man under such cultural pressure not to show his feelings even when his wife had died, I developed a new empathy with the opposite sex. It also became demonstrably clear over the rest of the scene that Brutus's grief did indeed cloud his judgment despite his stiff upper lip.

Boys' Toys

From this moment the play rushes headlong to its conclusion—at least it *should* rush. In many productions it plods. Scene changes and clunking armour slow the pace, and we sit and watch the swish, thunk, duck, swipe of well-toned, sweating actors grunting in fights to which we probably know the outcome.

We had plenty of athletic, well-toned women in our company, so it wasn't that we couldn't have staged these battles traditionally, but most of us switch off in those predictable battle scenes. Phyllida had always known she wanted music to play a large part in the production, so for our first time round in 2012/13* we had a brilliant drummer, an extraordinary Greek electric guitarist with a crimson streak in her hair, a bass guitarist who was also a comedy writer, and my servant Lucius, who was also a boxer and writer and played a mean saxophone.

In preparation for war, the drummer, dressed in combats and shades, sat on a raised movable platform with a single drum and started playing a low and steady drumroll. The rest of the cast raced on with different drums and cymbals and, as they were set up on the platform, the drummer added each sound into the build-up until an entire drum kit was assembled (presumably the prison had authorised the hire). The army then leapt on to the moving platform. Flashing lights and blasting electric guitars were added as it swirled around the space with soldiers falling to their deaths or leaping up to climb up the prison stairway frame. One critic wrote that he had seldom seen so much testosterone on a stage.

Our Clean Break friends pointed out that even for a play the inmates would not be allowed to use anything sharp that could be used as a weapon, so we used what would have been available to us; boys' toys from the prison nursery unit, i.e water-pistols and plastic machine guns. Put those in the hands of amateur actor/prisoners with the rare excuse to let off steam and we hoped to create an illusion of barely contained danger.

---

* At the time of writing we are about to remount the play with a different musical grouping.

Suicide

Robert Harris, the historian and novelist, came to talk to us during rehearsals. He endorsed the choice of our prison setting, pointing out that Rome was felt by many to be a prison. The conspirators were desperate and in such a climate they hint at suicide as an escape:

CASSIUS:
That part of tyranny that I do bear
I can shake off at pleasure.

CASCA:
So can I:
So every bondman in his own hand bears
The power to cancel his captivity

All of our prison cast could relate to this, especially Hannah as a lifer with no hope of release. Suicide is a complex issue, and I won't presume to plumb its depths here. I will just pick out a few strands.

Strand 1
Young women in prison who try to kill themselves because they see themselves as worthless. The world would be better off without them, they think.

Strand 2
Statistically suicide is most common among young men. Grayson Perry again, talking of a thirty-year-old man who had killed himself:

No one had a clue he was suicidal. I think some men don't even know when they are sad.

Strand 3
It was a Roman soldier's duty to fall on his sword in the event of defeat or failure. This involved getting someone else to hold that sword.

All these strands plaited together over the last beats of the play. Cassius, mistakenly thinking that Octavius has defeated

Brutus (in fact the opposite is true), gets his slave Pindarus to finish him off. When Messala finds his dead body he understands that '*Mistrust of good success hath done this deed*'.

When Brutus finds his dead friend, he knows who to blame:

> O Julius Caesar, thou art mighty yet!
> Thy spirit walks abroad and turns our swords
> In our own proper entrails.

Fear and guilt are eating into their morale and dooming them to lose the war. Is this Shakespeare's message? That regime change will ultimately fail? Hannah deeply hopes not. I hope Shakespeare is less decided than that and simply wants us to ask questions and learn about ourselves. He has engineered a trick of the plot in order to achieve tragedy, in order to teach us something. Just as *Romeo and Juliet* could have ended happily if Friar John had been able to get Friar Laurence's message through to Romeo, Cassius and Brutus might have lived to fight another battle had not Pindarus, on look-out, misread the situation he sees far off in Brutus's camp. Shakespeare doesn't alter the historical fact of Cassius's and Brutus's deaths, but he imagines them in such a way to make us aware of the 'it needn't have been like that' aspect. Our minds shape our destinies.

The thrash-metal sounds build throughout the last beat of the play, punctuating Brutus's speeches as he desperately seeks someone who will hold the sword for him to fall on, while he urges his friends to escape the advancing enemy: his last effort to salvage some good from the disaster.

> My heart doth joy that yet in all my life
> I found no man but he was true to me.
> I shall have glory by this losing day
> More than Octavius and Mark Antony
> By this vile conquest shall attain unto.

At this point I got to be a sort of rock performer in my sixties. Slap in the spotlight, my men dropping all around me, drums thrashing, lights flashing, an electric guitar wailing as Brutus does a kind of desperate dance trying to summon up the guts to shoot himself in the head (…with a water pistol). Finally he gets his servant Lucius (in the original it is one, Strato, whom we barely know) to do the deed. Lucius the boy soldier. Will he take Brutus's lessons to his heart or is he so brutalised by the war that he joins the winning side? The latter of course.

With Brutus safely dead, Mark Antony can afford a generous eulogy. Our Mark Antony speedily beckons to a 'camera man' to make sure it gets filmed for the nation. The PR will do him good. For a second *he* is the unifier we hoped Brutus would be, but, almost immediately, Octavius sweeps the carpet out from under him and assumes the cloak.

Frankie/Caesar, who has appeared at intermittent moments during the play, as Caesar's ghost appearing to Brutus on the eve of battle, and then during the battle itself, now sits at the drum-kit orchestrating all of this with single, startling drumbeats. We all move to her tune. I rise up and join the ranks again and then suddenly, just before we reach the end, a deafening blast comes from the prison tannoy: 'FIVE MINUTES TO LOCK-UP!'

A mixture of fury at being cut off in mid-flow and elation at their achievement runs through the prisoners. The flurry of reaction masks a surprising and shocking costume change. Frankie (ex-Caesar) has dropped her disguise and suddenly we see her dressed in the uniform of the prison officer she has been all along. She orders us into line ready to leave the space.

At this point we shed the Roman layer of the play within the play and were just actors playing prisoners. Each of these prisoners had given her all, had felt empowered by understanding Shakespeare's language and by having it on her tongue-tip. Now each prisoner was reduced to a number. Phyllida wanted Hannah to be the last to leave. She invited me to take my time, to do something distinct from the others. She wouldn't define it, and I never planned it. The challenge was to drop the acting and find Hannah's agony somewhere inside. I thought of Judith Clark. The same age as me, she has been locked away for thirty-five years. Yes, she made mistakes, but the only life she took was her own. Prison brought her time to think and to make a profound turnaround. Why is she still there?

Prison Officer Frankie broke my reverie and hurried me along, and, as the door clanged shut behind the cast, I hoped we had done *Julius Caesar* justice, but I also hoped that we had left the audience with a sense of the talent we waste when we sideline swathes of society or lock them out of sight.

HENRY IV

'Uneasy lies the head that wears a crown'

As King Henry IV
Henry IV, Donmar Warehouse, 2014

This was the second of what became the Donmar all-female Shakespeare trilogy. We performed at the Donmar Warehouse in 2014 and at St Ann's Warehouse in Brooklyn in 2015.

A Power of English

Supposing Brutus had not died, had won the war and had had a son. Suppose that son grew up to be a wastrel, uninterested in the price his father had paid to achieve power, and whose lifestyle made a nonsense of everything his father believed.

This is more or less the scenario with King Henry and his son Prince Hal.

I was now preparing a second female prison Shakespeare play, and so my usual desire to look for differences between the character I last played and the one I am about to play had to be set aside in the interests of developing the thematic links that enriched the prison plays. After all, in one way I was playing the same character, Hannah. She was my stepping stone to understanding both these men who had done damage and lived with remorse.

Elizabethan England was repairing itself after years of religious and tribal war, and Queen Elizabeth was striving to be the banner under which all factions could be united.

The same is true of King Henry, and one way to unite a nation is to create a common enemy. From the very opening of the play he sets out his aim. Civil war must end:

> No more the thirsty entrance of this soil
> Shall daub her lips with her own children's blood;

and

> Forthwith a power of English shall we levy;
> Whose arms were moulded in their mothers' womb
> To chase these pagans in those holy fields
> Over whose acres walk'd those blessed feet
> Which fourteen hundred years ago were nail'd
> For our advantage on the bitter cross.

(In fact I spoke a slightly streamlined version, taking the liberty of changing Shakespeare's rather confusing syntax so we were off to '*chase those pagans from the Holy Land*', iambic pentameter intact.)

The speech is a neat piece of emotional blackmail, invoking mothers and the martyred Jesus to secure loyalty to this King who had got the crown by dubious means.

The crowd rallies to him, stirred by the concept of their common Englishness.

Of the possible other plays on director Phyllida Lloyd's list, *Henry IV* lent itself best to an ensemble of players, giving decent parts to the most people. On the huge canvas of the *Henry IV* plays, Shakespeare seems to be asking the still relevant question: Who are we as a people? What binds us together?

In his time the country was in fact a mix of Scottish, Irish, Welsh and French, not to mention other foreigners and 'strangers' from continental Europe. Our twenty-first-century, all-female cast represented an even wider demographic and ethnic spread, all but two of us calling ourselves British. We demanded to be included in Shakespeare's discussion.

Right from the start, the sight of fourteen women coming on stage was in itself extraordinary. How do you categorise fourteen women? You can't. In a 'normal' play you might get three women and you might think, 'Oh I get it; she's the young innocent, she's the spoilt sexpot, she's the uptight secretary' or whatever. I exaggerate, of course, but you get the idea. Our cast was composed of women of all ages, sizes, colours and sexualities, some of African, some of Caribbean, Chinese or Indian descent, some Irish, some Scottish, one Spanish. Many were Shakespeare virgins, but each had a unique quality and skill to bring to the group. We had some wonderful musicians, some stand-up comedians, a poet and a DJ. Most of them would be playing more than one part: a man and a woman maybe, or an earl and a cutpurse.

The prison itself was the unifying factor in our play, and this gave us a particular advantage. Most productions strive for a uniformity of style, and are cast with a view to creating a coherent family or societal picture which can occasionally lead to a rather bland neutrality. The prison was our coherent stage world and could accommodate our variety.

Preparations

With Phyllida we spent hours unknotting the text, making sure we all understood it. We paraphrased speeches, delved into dictionaries, looked up references and shared all this round a table.

Barbara Houseman, our voice coach, convinced us that speaking this language was within the grasp of all of us. One of the main issues that came up was that of accent. The Irish, the Scottish, the South Londoners all felt that to drop their accent would make them feel inauthentic. It was agreed that we should each speak with our own accent, and the audience would just have to adjust to the idea that a young black woman from South London *was* Lord Mortimer, and a Spanish woman *was* Lord Northumberland.

I knew there were some in the group who looked to me as an experienced Shakespeare speaker, and I didn't want them trying to imitate me, so I announced rather sheepishly that RP—or whatever you want to call it—*was* my accent and that I didn't want to feel inauthentic either by 'putting on' some fake cockney. (In the event I did roughen up my accent. Henry became more mob leader than noble king.)

Britain is the only country I know where people are pre-judged by their accents before being judged for their pronouncements. One of our missions was to liberate actors and audiences alike from some preconceived idea of how Shakespeare's language should sound. The important thing was to make our speech and our intentions clear so we could deliver up the play, and that I think we achieved.

If you passionately believe in something and love it, you can either hug it to yourself or you want as many other people in the world to love it too to endorse your own belief. That is how I am about Shakespeare. That is why I cared so much that we did not alienate the young people and school-kids who came to the play. They saw people like themselves sounding like themselves, and it linked them into the play. It made them feel included.

The two parts of *Henry IV* are massive. Every echelon of English society is depicted, and the play roams all over the country. The complete version can last four or five hours. We needed it to run at two hours max, with no interval to break the tension.

So Phyllida judiciously cut the play, slicing out whole characters and bits of battle plot. The resulting script was mostly comprised of *Part I* but with cherry-picked best bits from *Part II* (Lady Percy's 'Go not to these wars' speech, the King's 'Uneasy lies the head' speech, the King's death and the final rejection of Falstaff).

This stripping down had the effect of highlighting the triangular central relationship between Falstaff, Hal and the King. Hal is torn between the fun of Falstaff, with his petty criminal gang at The Boar's Head, and his own ambition to be King. His first soliloquy shows that he has a game-plan to play along with the lowlife and fool the establishment into thinking he's a lost cause; then, like the prodigal son, he will be doubly treasured when he does return to the fold. Shakespeare had a game-plan too: to show a future King Henry V who knew his people first-hand, unlike his father.

Connections

A core of the cast had also been in *Julius Caesar*. Clare Dunne, who had played my wife Portia, was now playing my son Prince Hal. In the New York version of *Henry IV*, Henry's chief enemy Lord Worcester was played by Jenny Jules, who had played Cassius. This gave us an opportunity to enrich the subtext between our characters. Worcester, like Cassius, had been a co-conspirator against the previous ruler and was now feeling slighted and excluded by an increasingly remote King. Might not the brotherly love between Cassius and Brutus have turned sour if they had survived to run Rome?

In prison, strong emotional attachments are made and suddenly destroyed by some random relocation or because one prisoner is set free and the other remains. Again I thought of Judith Clark (see Chapter Nine on Brutus), whose whole world is confined in one building and who has formed close bonds with women who come and then go. Like Judith, Hannah would have developed defences against the pain of this.

I went to an all-girls' boarding school, which meant being away from my family for many months on end. It is a frivolous comparison, but I do understand how, away from home, you become more emotionally dependent on the people in your immediate environment than on your family, and how you develop strategies to survive among your peers.

This was the only personal connection I had to draw on to imagine life in prison. Other members of the cast had closer links to the sort of women they were playing. One had been in prison herself. Some had had problems with addiction and mental illness, some were mothers of small children and could imagine that most awful separation forced on so many women prisoners with all the worry for those children's future it entails—another reason why we should think several times before giving mothers custodial sentences for low-grade, drug-related crimes or prostitution.

The actors playing Falstaff and Hal had done workshops in two prisons in Yorkshire before rehearsals began and had learnt which of the play's themes resonated most with the inmates. In the tussle over Hal's future they saw a familiar story of a drug pusher (Falstaff) exploiting a younger person's (Hal's) dependency on drugs in order to keep them in the prison and under their control, while another senior role model (Henry) is fighting for that same person to get clean and take up a life outside.

Thanks to the prisoners' input, we adopted this story as our subtext. Hannah, the mentor who had perhaps kicked a drug habit herself, wanted for Donna/Hal the future she had lost for herself. Andrea/Falstaff offered a far more attractive route at first but an ultimately destructive one. Within this context, Hal's first speech seemed to be that of an overconfident addict fooling themselves and promising us (the audience, or a parole board?) that they have the habit under control.

> I'll so offend, to make offence a skill;
> Redeeming time when men think least I will.

We invented a set-up before the play proper began, whereby Donna had just been given parole. Now the stakes were extremely high for Andrea and Hannah. This subtext would not and should not be made explicit to the audience, but it gave extra fuel and commitment to our performances.

Scene Changes

Another theme that the prison visits threw up was that of territory, the need for space in a crowded, noisy place where no one respects privacy. One room can be used by a religious group for an hour, then be turned over to a yoga group or a therapy session. The staff might grudgingly sanction these group activities outside the cell, but sessions could be broken up at any moment. This fed into the territorial wars between the factions in *Henry IV.*

With our choreographer Ann Yee (who is much more than a choreographer) we followed through the work we had done on *Julius Caesar* exploring crowd dynamics and now worked on gang dynamics. Playing men was not so much about putting on deep voices or blokeish walks; it was more about stripping away feminine gestures. We found so many of our female cultural habits (softening our voices, folding ourselves into neat shapes, 'explaining' things with hand movements) were about accommodating other people and making ourselves less threatening. We tried to get into a mindset of entitlement: entitlement to be seen and heard, to take up space and dominate a room. This confidence led us to a simpler, more direct body language.

Hotspur, Worcester, Northumberland and his gang were dubbed by us the 'gym bunnies'. It suited their dedication and preparedness for war compared with Hal's dissipation. They brought on gym equipment for their scenes and discussed their rebel plans while working out. The actresses themselves were extremely fit, and it was wonderful to watch school*boys* in the audience agape with wonder that women could do ten consecutive pull-ups on a bar.

A blast of music from our DJ/actor and a quick scene change: gym mats rolled up, benches moved to the side and The Boar's Head was put together. On the principle that we could only use what was easily available in the prison, the pub furniture came from the nursery area. Little coloured plastic chairs and tables, a plastic toy 'shop' for the bar, plastic cups for tankards, etc. These scenes were mostly joyously funny, with Falstaff entertaining his onstage audience, grabbing a mic and serenading Hal with a blast of 'Gimme money... that's what I want', dressed in the faux-fur coat and blonde wig they had stolen from me (yes me, alias 'a pilgrim' or American tourist in what had become a carjack scene in place of the ambush at Gadshill). I was also allowed to put on a beanie and join in the pub fun, witnessing at close hand (and in slight pain) Falstaff's imitation of the King.

Next up we whisked the audience to Wales for the Glendower scene. I helped clear the plastic furniture, put on a hoodie and joined one of the three gangs that stood behind Hotspur, Mortimer and Glendower. Our job was to back our leader in all things.

The scene had barely begun when, in a wonderfully naturalistic moment, Shakespeare has Hotspur say,

A plague upon it! I have forgot the map,

whereupon various of us rushed out with spray cans of different colours and painted a huge outline of England and Wales on the floor. We then placed three signs, 'England', 'Wales' and 'to Scotland', in their appropriate spots.

With Glendower's grandstanding and Hotspur's undercutting, it is one of the funniest scenes in the play. With women in the roles we could highlight the preposterousness of certain aspects of male behaviour, as we grunted approval behind our respective gang leader, arms folded over huge imagined chests, legs spread wide.

I am sure Shakespeare was on our side. Surely he meant to send up the whole idea of carving up and dishing out bits of a country in this boys' playground squabble...

HOTSPUR:
Methinks my portion, north from Burton here,
In quantity equals not one of yours:
See how this river comes me cranking in,
And cuts me from the best of all my land...
I'll have the current in this place damm'd up...
It shall not wind with such a deep indent.

GLENDOWER:
Not wind? it shall, it must; you see it doth.

MORTIMER:
Yea, but mark how he bears his course, and runs me up
With like advantage on the other side;
Gelding the opposed continent as much
As on the other side it takes from you

...so we considered ourselves licensed to do silly things. The scene ends in reconciliation and manly claps on backs. Then Glendower enjoins the men to say goodbye to their women:

There will be a world of water shed
Upon the parting of your wives and you.

Spoken with a twinkle in his/Jackie Clune's eye. (Women, eh?)
The silly mood is broken by Lady Percy singing a beautiful contemporary pop song, 'Daddy's Gone', in place of the Welsh Lady's song of the original. It was a poignant contrast to the hilarity we had just been part of, a reminder of centuries of women left behind when their husbands go to war. The sudden switch of mood was Shakespeare's idea not ours. We were hopefully aiding his intentions by having all the prison women enter the space, stripped of pretence (well, one layer of it), and curl up on the floor to sleep, or try to. Each woman seemed mentally isolated as when locked in her cell alone to face her demons.

Insomnia

When the song ended, I appeared on an upper level as King Henry, kept awake by anxiety for his kingship. Sleeplessness in Shakespeare's characters is often about guilt, but he gives his '*guilty creatures*' some of his most beautiful words as they long for sleep.

From Macbeth:

> the innocent sleep,
> Sleep that knits up the ravell'd sleeve of care,
> The death of each day's life [etc.]

and from Henry in our play:

> O gentle sleep,
> Nature's soft nurse, how have I frighted thee,
> That thou no more wilt weigh my eyelids down
> And steep my senses in forgetfulness?

Phyllida airlifted this speech from *Part II* and placed it here, with Henry looking down with envy on his subjects, whom he supposes can have nothing to worry about. Incidentally, in a later prison workshop this scene was picked out by some of the real inmates as one they could particularly relate to. I found it remarkable that they saw past the elitist figure of a King to a fellow human being plagued by insomnia and anxiety.

There is a loneliness at the heart of Henry. In our stripped-down cast, he appeared with only two or three loyal supporters rather than a full court, and he missed out on all the fun.

He is getting old and worries about his legacy, which his heir seems hell-bent on wrecking. He had a brief moment of popularity with the crowd at the top of the play, but almost immediately after that he learns that rebellion has reared its head again, and the idea of a pilgrimage to Jerusalem must be postponed. All his best intentions are dragged back into war.

Shakespeare is not concerned with the real Henry. He is a playwright not a historian, and unapologetically bends historical characters to fit the story he wants to tell. In *Richard II* he shows the same character, then plain Henry Bolingbroke, as the popular saviour of the country, a counterweight to the increasingly despotic Richard. Now for the purposes of his argument Richard is '*that sweet lovely rose*' and was supplanted by '*this thorn, this canker, Bolingbroke*'.

What Shakespeare does seem interested in is the internal moral dilemma of a ruler who has been compelled to do bad things in order to survive. I have already mentioned the echo of Elizabeth I, and I wonder, if she saw the play, whether she would have taken any comfort from the speech's seemingly empathetic last line: '*Uneasy lies the head that wears a crown.*'

At the end of the sleep speech, Hal tiptoes in as if creeping back from a late night at the tavern. Wakeful Henry pounces on him and harangues him. Henry is not a likeable man. To him likeability is a luxury. He may even be a little jealous of the decadent but convivial life his son leads.

Hal's reactions under fire range from defiant to abject. Henry tries several tactics to engage his son. The scene is very alive if you play it moment by moment, each of you reacting slightly differently to the other's slightly different reactions every night. Of course, a lot of Hal's reactions are unspoken, but as Henry you learn to read the signs. You can pick up hints in both men's speeches that they desperately want one another's love, but at this point there is not enough trust between them to do more than hint.

Henry can't confide his doubts about how he got the crown, and Hal can't explain why he needs the love of Falstaff to fill the gap left by his father's coldness. Honesty will come later, when it is almost too late.

There are always key lines that an actor grabs hold of as pointing to the deepest core of a character. One such for me was Henry's line to Hal:

The hope and expectation of thy time
Is ruin'd.

It contained something of Brutus's energy when he cries out
to Cassius:

Remember March, the ides of March remember:
Did not great Julius bleed for justice' sake?

Both lines carry the question, 'What was it all for? Was it
worth it if you are going to let the whole thing slide?'

Hal has heard it all before and behaves like a hangdog ado-
lescent. Where Henry can get him is on the subject of
Hotspur. By holding Hotspur up as the perfect, brave young
man committed to war and victory, and by means of a sarcastic twist ('*Thou art like enough, to fight against me under
Percy's pay*'), he goads Hal into action.

Hal vows that:

I shall make this northern youth exchange
His glorious deeds for my indignities.
And I will call him to so strict account,
That he shall render every glory up...
Or I will tear the reckoning from his heart.

At last Hal is on side, even if not quite for the reasons Henry
had hoped. It will do for now.

A Lame Attempt at Peace

From Henry's point of view, he has been forced into this war
just when he hoped to heal the nation and move on. His old
sins and Worcester's old wounds won't lie down quietly. Perhaps he senses he is not long for this world and needs to
control the narrative of his times. Why can't bygones be
bygones?

He comes together with his enemies to parley. Like many
guilty people, Henry blames others. In his book Worcester

has a choice to pull back from a war that will bring a *'broachéd mischief to the unborn times'*.

This was a tricky line. Firstly, what is *'broachéd'*? Secondly, *'mischief'* doesn't quite cover the idea that the fallout from war blights several generations to come. It was frustrating to have such an important point wrapped in an opaque package. I changed *'broachéd'* to *'curséd'*, which helped a bit, but I was stuck with *'mischief'*.

The scene does not go Henry's way. His rather sanctimonious overture is quickly subverted as Worcester nabs the moral high ground, listing his family's grievances. Henry quietly fumes, and in our production I lost control and threw the furniture at my enemy in a display of macho indignation.

Hal steps in to calm things down, offering a way out of the impasse. He offers to fight Hotspur in single combat and save thousands of lives. Henry can't accept that. He thinks Hal doesn't stand a chance against the super-fit Hotspur, and besides, for all Henry's arguments against war, he knows he has to fight and needs to win.

Moving Like a Man

I have to confess to having rather enjoyed strutting and striding and puffing out my chest. I suspect that many men enjoy it too. I have watched those sorts of men all my life, never thinking I would need those observations for an acting job. Since I was very young I have been able to watch someone and imagine myself inside them, moving their limbs, striking their poses and by some strange mechanism, getting an inkling as to their feelings and thoughts. I'm sure everyone has something of this ability, but it is particularly developed in actors. It is hard to explain how it's done because it is not a systematised process; it is just part of our equipment. It means that we can 'channel' someone from real life who matches the character we are playing.

As Henry, I channelled two or three different men (not the men themselves but their acting personae). For obvious reasons I had never had cause to channel Ray Winstone before, but I did now. Another model was Tom Bell; another was the guy from the film *A Prophet*, Niels Arestrup. If you know any of these actors, you will understand I was not striving to be a lookalike, but somehow, by keeping them in my mind's eye, I could borrow some useful quality of theirs: the stillness that accompanies physical power, the prowling pace of a man keeping his violence in check, the spread-limbed arrogance of those men on the tube who occupy two seats and leave you squished up in the corner.

It is a bit of a cliché to say it, but in many ways we are all acting. We have all been trained up in our physicality and raised within gender conventions that restrict us. The experiment of being a woman playing a man produced in me a hybrid that surprised me and released me from myself. That is what a lot of actors love best about the whole game—the escape from the limits of the package we are wrapped in. I suspect many non-actors are looking for the same.

The Woman Underneath

While the audience very quickly accepted that we women *were* the men we were pretending to be, there were times when it was effective to remind the audience of the female layer underneath.

The premise behind our prison convention was that the inmates had an input as to how to present certain scenes in a way that meant something to them. 'They' made choices such as giving Hotspur and Lady Percy a baby (a doll) which started bawling as soon as Hotspur picked it up. The woman playing Hotspur handed over this stinking alien thing to another woman playing Lady Percy. Then there was the moment when Hotspur, while ordering his little wifey to stay out of important things like battles, gets his jacket zip stuck and needs her help to fix it. These moments caused much laughter of recognition from the women in the audience.

In Act III, Scene 3, the inmates chose to bring out the misogyny in Falstaff and his gang as they round on the Hostess with what have usually been played as jokey Shakespearean insults. In an improvisation during rehearsals, the group came up with some really degrading contemporary sexist taunts and slung them at the Hostess. The inmate playing the part was in for prostitution. The boundary became unclear to this prison character with the result that she became upset and stopped the scene. We kept it in the play. The audience was never sure whether the Donmar actor had 'broken out', or whether she was acting the part of an inmate/prostitute who was breaking out.

After the parley between Henry and Worcester, the testosterone builds towards war, and here Falstaff delivers his famous anti-heroic '*catechism*' on the subject of honour:

> What is honour?… Who hath it? He that died o'
> Wednesday. Doth he feel it? No… 'Tis insensible then?
> Yea to the dead. But will it not live with the living? No…
> [etc.]

It is a deliberately subversive speech and sits well in a woman's voice. How many women have suffered and are still suffering because of a male notion of honour?

These were just some of the added layers of meaning that the women managed to excavate to make this giant play something to do with them.

We Go into Battle

We wanted no girly fighting or embarrassing sword-play. Our fight director Kate Waters was a keen boxer and, together with our movement wizard Ann Yee, created a brilliant choreographed battle of boxers. During the fighting when the Douglas threatens to kill the King, Hal steps in to save his father's life. We cut Shakespeare's dialogue and instead marked the moment with looks that seemed to say, 'I didn't know you cared' and 'See, I am not as useless as you thought'. Then the battle rushed to its climax: the showdown between Hal and Hotspur.

Both Jade Anouka (Hotspur) and Clare Dunne (Hal) trained enough to be convincing boxers. An abstract soundtrack punctuated their punches, and we lined the ring cheering and baying for blood. Again the sight of women doing this set the violence in greater relief than in most 'normal' male productions where the fighting is taken for granted.

Hotspur dies, the war is won, and Henry dishes out his punishments. Worcester and Vernon must die. Hal interrupts and pleads for the right to take care of the Douglas, and Henry agrees. His son has earned it. When Hal chooses to release the Douglas, because

> His valour shown upon our crests to-day
> Hath taught us how to cherish such high deeds
> Even in the bosom of our adversaries,

Henry again sees Hal in a new light. Perhaps this young man has lessons for us all? Perhaps he can be King and a greater King than I have been? It is the beginning of a process of letting go.

Legacy

Henry is dying, and Hal comes to visit him in inappropriately boisterous mood. The rebels have been vanquished! The King is asleep, so his attendants shush Prince Hal and invite him to leave the room. Hal refuses and stays alone watching over the King.

The audience eavesdrops on Hal's musings:

> Why doth the crown lie there upon his pillow,
> Being so troublesome a bedfellow?
> O polish'd perturbation! golden care!
> That keep'st the ports of slumber open wide
> To many a watchful night!

So he *does* understand. He *has* thought about kingship. Then he stops. He sees a feather near his father's nostrils which does not move.

> My gracious lord! my father!
> This sleep is sound indeed.

The insomniac King seems to have reached his final rest.

The audience sees Hal's genuine grief at what he supposes is his father's death. They see the solemnity with which he now puts on the crown. But Henry has missed all this. He wakes and misinterprets what he sees:

> Dost thou so hunger for mine empty chair
> That thou wilt needs invest thee with my honours
> Before thy hour be ripe?

Hal leaps out of his skin, as do some of the audience. Without giving Hal any chance to explain, Henry launches a devastating attack, unleashing all the fury and pain that has built up over years with as much force as his weak frame can muster. It is a whirlwind of a speech and technically tricky because you need maximum lung power while still convincing as a dying man. Henry is all the more desperate because he had begun to believe in his son and now feels he was fooled.

He bitterly charges Hal to

> dig my grave thyself,
> And bid the merry bells ring to thine ear
> That thou art crowned, not that I am dead...
> Give him that gave thee life unto the worms.
> Pluck down my officers, break my decrees.

That last line again made me think of Obama as he comes to the end of his second term. In his shoes I would be desperate to hand on the baton to someone who would complete the work I had set out to do, and fulfil any promises I had made but not delivered. What agony to imagine all of that falling away and handing the future to your enemy.

When Henry collapses for long enough, Hal defends himself wonderfully and honestly, and, though he doesn't say so in as many words, Henry gets the message that finally his son loves him.

In the nick of time the two men are reconciled. Henry gasps out his last, albeit oblique, confession,

> God knows, my son,
> By what by-paths and indirect crook'd ways
> I met this crown,

his blessing,

> And now my death
> Changes the mood; for what in me was purchased,
> Falls upon thee in a more fairer sort,

and some advice:

> Yet, though thou stand'st more sure than I could do,
> Thou art not firm enough... Therefore, my Harry,
> Be it thy course to busy giddy minds
> With foreign quarrels; that action, hence borne out,
> May waste the memory of the former days.

We have come full circle to that all too familiar political tactic of using war abroad to distract people from their grievances at home. It is advice that Henry V takes to heart.

Old Henry dies at peace with himself and God. If there had been doubts about his own right to rule, at least his son is a legitimate heir and the Plantagenet dynasty is secure.

As I lay in a nightshirt on a narrow prison hospital bed I was stripped of my manly accoutrements, and the scene sometimes felt like a mother/daughter scene as much as a father/son one. It also felt like Hannah saying goodbye to Donna, secure in the knowledge that she was going out into the world and would make a life for herself.

Andrea/Falstaff will not let go so happily. Donna/Hal next appears in the final scene at the top of a ladder repeating the first few lines of Henry's opening speech (a little liberty Phyllida took for emphasis). The crowd cheers and church bells ring. The Cheapside gang, with football rattles in celebratory mood, are ranged behind a police cordon. Fully confident that his own sweet King Hal will endow him with special favours for evermore, Falstaff calls out to him. Hal orders an officer to have him silenced and then delivers his devastating rejection:

> I know thee not old man. Fall to thy prayers.

By this time I had re-entered the stage as Hannah and joined the ranks of policemen. I felt a bit like Henry's ghost witnessing the triumph of my son as well as Hannah proudly watching her protégée playing her star role.

During Hal's speech, Andrea's Falstaff began to unravel. The untrained prison actor was unable to separate pretence from reality. The rejection was too real. She started to behave unpredictably. We all watched closely, ready to pounce if necessary, and then Andrea ran at the base of the ladder shouting desperately to Donna not to leave her. The prison guards rushed on and barked at us to lie on the floor. Andrea was grabbed and manacled and dragged screaming offstage. The rest of us silently obeyed the order to get up and stand in line. I tried to calm Donna down and make sure she didn't blow her parole by breaking out in some way, and we shuffled off. An ignominious end to our hard-fought-for play...

...But Not the End for Us

The two all-female Shakespeare plays that Phyllida and the Donmar had produced and which we had taken into schools, prisons and toured to St Ann's Warehouse in Brooklyn, New York, had started a buzz, and people were asking about a third. It was becoming known as a trilogy even before we had decided what play to do next.

After much thought and discussion we decided on *The Tempest*. This seemed a great throughline for Hannah/me. If Brutus was about getting power, and Henry was about holding on to power, Prospero would be about letting go of power.

The Tempest is Shakespeare's most experimental play. It is his and Prospero's swansong. It is a play about creativity itself. It is about imagination and control, about projection, about parenthood, possessiveness and forgiveness—so many things.

For over thirty years I have grown up through and alongside Shakespeare's characters. I have learnt things from them and put back what I have learnt into the playing of them. Prospero lets go of his anger, releases his prisoners Caliban and Ariel, sends his daughter out into the future and forgives his former enemies. He hands power over to the next generation. I am not quite ready to drown my book or break my staff, but I have a lot to learn about this next phase of life. I must prepare.

Epilogue

D̲ear Will (if I may),

You told us that (my emphasis)

> All the world's a stage,
> And all the men *and women* merely players:

but then you went on...

> And *one man* in *his* time plays many parts,
> *His* acts being seven ages.

Apart from the puking infant's nurse and the mistress's eye-brow, we women don't get a look-in. In most of your plays you seem to run out of women's ages once we have got our man. Up to that point you give us such wise and witty things to say and, particularly if we are wearing breeches, you even let us drive the plot, but in the final scene you have us knuckle down to marriage. Then what? Is that where the fun stops?

I am now what you would consider a very old woman, and I have felt somewhat starved of your material for the last ten to fifteen years. We seem only to be allowed into your stories as the daughters, mothers, wives or widows of the Main Man. Are you just not interested in our lives? I so want to be included in your wise humanistic embrace.

You said that the purpose of a play was '*to hold, as 'twere, the mirror up to nature*', but your own mirror doesn't reflect many women. That's half the population to a large extent obscured. I do appreciate that you were a jobbing playwright with a living to earn and that, in your day, women weren't allowed on the stage, and I also understand that women (*pace* your Queen) were not allowed at the centre of public life, so why would female characters feature at the centre of the drama that holds the mirror up to that public life? So you do have an excuse, but because you were such a genius, we are still doing your plays four hundred years after your death, and, because your words are still the highest form of expression of our human condition, we still swallow your plots and your social attitudes even though they don't fit us any more.

Dear William, *because* you are so famous and wonderful, you have cast a long shadow over the theatrical tradition, and despite the fact that the world has changed enormously since your day, the stories we tell about ourselves still tend to follow your template, with male protagonists whose thoughts and actions matter—and females who only matter in as much as they relate to those men.

I feel churlish for saying this, but many of us feel excluded, and I would love you to come back and do some rewrites.

Nowadays we are challenging all preconceptions about gender, both in terms of personal identification and public roles, so I hope you don't mind but I have been playing men recently. I am only following your own example. It seems as legitimate for women to play men as it was for boys to play women.

My function in the story is no longer constrained by my gender, and I am freed up to play out the general political and moral dilemmas that concern us all.

You have to understand that as Brutus I get to say things like:

There is a tide in the affairs of men,
Which, taken at the flood, leads on to fortune;
Omitted, all the voyage of their life
Is bound in shallows and in miseries,

while my wife Portia has speeches like:

Am I yourself
But, as it were, in sort or limitation,
To keep with you at meals, comfort your bed,
And talk to you sometimes? Dwell I but in the suburbs
Of your good pleasure? If it be no more
Portia is Brutus's harlot, not his wife,

which is perfectly brilliant, of course, but can you see that the speech itself is *about* limitation and that Portia defines her 'self' (as opposed to herself) wholly in relation to her husband or her father?

The women in your plays often have a moral clarity that comes from their very exclusion. Being outside the violence, they can comment on it. They can foresee the consequences but are helpless to prevent them from happening. You put their case so beautifully and eloquently, but once they have had their say (usually in one scene) you remove us from the play, and we have to spend the rest of the evening in our dressing room.

As Brutus I felt so privileged to play a character whose main concerns were freedom, power, morality and mortality. You may be shocked to see women playing men in battle and murdering their leader—and it was somehow saddening for us that we could ape their behaviour so convincingly—but it served to sharpen the question: Is there another way? I wonder if your amazing imagination and understanding of humanity could come up with a new and better path for us.

In many parts of the world the attitude to women has not changed since your day, but we are all trying. We women talk amongst ourselves about politics and philosophy, and many now take an active part on the world stage. We have several women leaders running important countries. Where I live, people from all continents, races, cultures and religions move amongst one another, intermarry and exchange ideas—admittedly not always peaceably but more successfully than the newsmongers or cynical politicians would have us believe.

There is now a thing called the Bechdel test devised by a woman in America which requires that a script fulfils three criteria:

1. There should be at least two women in it (you tick that box)
2. Who talk to one another... (you tick that one too, but pretty seldom)
3. (and here's the catch)... about something besides a man.

Off the top of my head I cannot think of one example of that in your work. With Olivia and Viola the subject is Orsino. Emilia tells Desdemona all about men. With the Countess of Rousillon and Helena, it's Bertram. With Rosalind and Celia, it's Orlando. When Hero and her women get together in an all-female enclave you can only imagine them talking about wedding dresses. Ah! I can think of one: Princess Katherine and Alice in *Henry V* have an English lesson, although you could say the reason for learning is to get a man.

I am being hard on you, particularly as so many writers now do no better. I just wonder what you would write for us now.

You see, imitating men can't be the only answer either on the stage or the world stage.

Dear Will, when I speak your words I feel I am having a private conversation with a friend today who is whispering eternal truths in my ear. Four hundred years after your death we are still acting out your stories all over the world in every conceivable situation and in every conceivable language. As you foretold in Sonnet 18, your words will resonate '*so long as men can breathe or eyes can see*'. Being the most famous Englishman that ever lived you prove the pen to be mightier than the sword, and you give dignity to my profession. All the world is indeed a stage, and I cannot imagine a world without you. I just wish you had put more women at the centre of your world/stage. Our stories matter not because of our relation to men but because we are members of the human race. To be or not to be, that is a question for us all.

Your ever loving,
Harriet

A Chronology of Shakespearean Performances

1974   Octavia in *Antony and Cleopatra*, Duke's
        Playhouse, Lancaster

1980   Ophelia in *Hamlet*, Royal Court Theatre,
        London

1981–3 Helena in *A Midsummer Night's Dream*, and
        Helena in *All's Well That Ends Well*, Royal
        Shakespeare Company, Stratford-upon-Avon
        and Barbican, London (and *All's Well* at the
        Martin Beck Theater, Broadway, New York)

1982–3 Lady Percy in *Henry IV, Parts I and II*, Royal
        Shakespeare Company, Barbican, London

1982   Olivia in *Twelfth Night*, and Juliet in *Romeo
        and Juliet*, BBC Radio 4

1987   Portia in *The Merchant of Venice*, Royal
        Exchange Theatre, Manchester

1987–9 Viola in *Twelfth Night*, and Imogen in
        Cymbeline, Royal Shakespeare Company,
        Stratford-upon-Avon and Barbican, London

1997   Hermione in *The Winter's Tale*, BBC Radio 4

1998   Tamora in *Titus Andronicus*, Arkangel
        Shakespeare (audiobook)

1999–2000 Lady Macbeth in *Macbeth*, Royal Shakespeare Company, Stratford-upon-Avon, and Young Vic, London; USA and Japan tour; and Illuminations Films

2002 Beatrice in *Much Ado About Nothing*, Royal Shakespeare Company, Stratford-upon-Avon, and Theatre Royal Haymarket, London; Goneril in *King Lear* with Paul Scofield, Naxos AudioBooks

2006–7 Cleopatra in *Antony and Cleopatra*, Royal Shakespeare Company, Stratford-upon-Avon, and Novello Theatre, London; USA tour

2007 Maria in *Twelfth Night*, Houghton Hall for Norwich Theatre Royal

2012–13 Brutus in *Julius Caesar*, Donmar Warehouse, London; St Ann's Warehouse, Brooklyn, New York City (revived at Donmar King's Cross, London, in 2016)

2014–15 Henry IV in *Henry IV*, Donmar Warehouse, London; St Ann's Warehouse, Brooklyn, New York City (revived at Donmar King's Cross, London, in 2016)

2016–17 Prospero in *The Tempest*, Donmar King's Cross, London; St Ann's Warehouse, Brooklyn, New York City

www.nickhernbooks.co.uk

facebook.com/nickhernbooks

twitter.com/nickhernbooks